PREDATOR

PREDATOR

A MEMOIR, A MOVIE, AN OBSESSION

ANDER MONSON

GRAYWOLF PRESS

This publication is made possible, in part, by the voters of Minnesota through a Minnesota State Arts Board Operating Support grant, thanks to a legislative appropriation from the arts and cultural heritage fund. Significant support has also been provided by the McKnight Foundation, the Lannan Foundation, the Amazon Literary Partnership, and other generous contributions from foundations, corporations, and individuals. To these organizations and individuals we offer our heartfelt thanks.

Published by Graywolf Press
212 Third Avenue North, Suite 485
Minneapolis, Minnesota 55401

www.graywolfpress.org

Published in the United States of America

ISBN 978-1-64445-200-4 (paperback)
ISBN 978-1-64445-184-7 (ebook)

2 4 6 8 9 7 5 3 1
First Graywolf Printing, 2022

Library of Congress Control Number: 2022930739

Cover design: Adam Bohannon

For Megan and for Paul Monette
and for all the boys I've been before

CONTENTS

PREDATOR

Seeing Stars

I ALWAYS FORGET ABOUT THIS PREAMBLE, in which we start our journey from space into the jungle and through action into horror. But here we are, seeing stars. A whole wild field of them. Then "Schwarzenegger," then "PREDATOR," and—my Fitbit tells me, "Fat burn!"—my pulse is already racing. The camera pans down slowly to more space. Enter a spaceship that looks a little wonky, but not bad for the '80s, presumably done with models. This is among the worst effects the movie will have to offer. There's a planet: Earth, we guess. The spaceship spawns a little something that looks like a space sperm, and it goes off toward the planet. We see it enter the atmosphere in a dash of orange.

I've watched *Predator* 146 times, and this part always surprises me when I put it on again, because it's so odd and disconnected from the rest of the movie. It provides a frame, I guess, to the action that will come, but it definitely does not feel essential. It really wants to let us know there's an ALIEN in this movie, that this is about SPACE, not only cool dudes in the jungle. It's a bizarre way to open one of the most influential, iconic, and interesting action movies of all time.

John McTiernan, the film's director, forgot about it, too, as he tells us in the director's commentary for the fifteenth anniversary DVD. This whole bit was added after shooting, he tells us, and it's possible he's never actually *seen* it, he says. That's how little he remembers it. First, though, he complains about the 20th Century Fox logo: it's distorted, he wants us to know, because he wasn't allowed to shoot the film in anamorphic widescreen because the studio wouldn't let him on account of some technical aspect of the visual effects. I don't quite care enough about what that means exactly to track it down, but he still seems bitter about it, fifteen years later. He had a lot of conflicts with the studio making this movie. This was the first big studio film he'd directed after his first movie, an ambitious but low-budget horror flick called *Nomads* (starring an often shirtless future James Bond, Pierce Brosnan, in his first movie role). Making *Predator*, McTiernan tells us in a voice that can only be described as soporific, allowed him to make all his other movies, including *Die Hard*, his other action classic, and a whole string of movies you may recognize: *The Hunt for Red October, Last Action Hero, The Thomas Crown Affair*, among others. I'm watching *Predator* again with him for the fifteenth anniversary. And I'm watching the movie with you because you need to watch it. I mean, we're watching it already. The world we're living in watched it and consumed it, and now I see it everywhere I go.

I wish I didn't have to see it. I feel like I saw enough dudes with guns in the 1980s and 1990s for a lifetime. Or, rather, I wish I could watch those dudes only on-screen, where they can only do on-screen damage, but those dudes are now increasingly on the screen every time I watch not movies but the news. They pose a threat: it was obvious then (that's the whole point of this movie we're watching, after all), but watch them pour into the United States Capitol Building on January 6, 2021, in Washington, DC, and tell me it's just a movie.

CAN WE DIVINE A CULTURE FROM ITS FILMS, especially the ones that stick? Some cops get shot, I think of *Predator*. Some cops shoot kids. Guns in the grocery store, I think of Dutch, Schwarzenegger's character. A firework burns down a neighbor's house and I think SFX. A sexual predator's elected I call him predator when I call him anything. I call him *yours*. I call him also mine because even though I might resent a thing it still claims me against my will. Another Black man is killed by the police I think of *Predator*. Another. Another. My congresswoman gets shot outside a Safeway supermarket a bike ride from my house. A nine-year-old is killed, along with five others. It's awful. A good guy with a gun fails to stop a bad guy with a gun in time, I wish for fiction. I keep reloading in the games I play and am annoyed to even have to make such a minor gesture toward realism. Predator and other drones fly low in foreign lands I cannot forget. "Civilian casualties"—words that hide atrocities—I think of it. On the disc golf course one dude joyfully cries out a line from the film ("Get to the choppa!") I respond, in my best Schwarzeneggerian accent, "Kill me! Kill me now! Come on!" without thinking.

Only a little later I think of what that interaction meant. How quickly I was roused to respond! How well I know all these lines. How often I've seen the movie, and what I proved by watching it.

It is a good time to invest in guns in America. It is always a good time to invest in guns in America. It will not change until the guns are gone or we are. I am from Michigan, a land of guns, after all, and now I live in another one: Arizona. I might be half a country away from home, ringed by cholla and saguaro, not mile-tall pines, but my uneasy feeling that everybody's armed doesn't change.

I'm menaced by a cop. I fear traffic stops. I know it's not the same—my white skin my Subaru my bad haircut my indie rock speak for me already.

Some things eat inside of you—as if you've been impregnated by an alien. It's been more than thirty years since *Predator*. It's as if I exist to be a catalyst for this, this movie filling me, embiggening me. It's on-screen light I'm seeing, not even the record of the thing itself but a secondary trace. This film is thirty years old but it still feels hot, watching it. Cosplayers meet online and at conventions to reenact scenes and compare the detail of their sculpts, not to say their sculpted abs, though that might happen in private later. The Predator Masters convention meets a few miles from my home at the International Wildlife Museum, I think of *Predator*. They are an online hunting club whose members specialize in killing "apex" predators such as coyotes and lions and bears and lynx with all kinds of expensive gear they sell to each other to dress up in and tote around.

Guns in classrooms and in bars, you know what I'm thinking. Redneck in a truck threatening to kick someone's ass for some perceived infraction at the farmer's market: *Predator*. Open carry, no permit required, on campus, in my classroom: sure, let's all pack Glocks and shotguns up on racks. If you've seen the movie, then you know that when we're all armed, we're all targets all the time. Not only for each other either. The alien won't attack the unarmed or the weak for lack of sport. For instance, it spares the woman, whose role is to be a contrast to the boys. It spares another woman in the sequel because she's pregnant and disarmed. Unlike us the creature won't kill a kid. Is carrying a defense or is it not, and against what I am not sure. We're not as big and fast as we think we are. At Tucson's Sabino Canyon hiking with my wife I see a sign informing us not to try to pick up rattlesnakes. "Picking up a rattlesnake is not a test of your strength or speed or skill," the sign says, though of course it is, a dumb one. Those bitten by rattlesnakes are 95 percent likely to be men, aged fifteen to twenty-five, struck on the hands or face.

I mean, I understand how it feels to shoot the rush the after-strut the feeling bigger the sense of safety that parenthesis of empowerment that we can use to fix ourselves in grammar. A subject has to have a predicate for the sentence to work right. When we shoot we must shoot *at*. Even when we're firing into nothing it's never really nothing.

The feeling, not the plot, drives the action in *Predator*. That feeling is a lot. Yes, that we're allowed. My congresswoman Gabrielle Giffords is shot and first we believe she's dead and then alive but barely. A year goes by she speaks, but she is not the same. My most satisfying response that year was to play first-person shooter games in which I prefer to fire from range with sniper rifles, head shots obviously, like the congresswoman got: spooky action from a distance. It's awful to be feeling it balancing out like this but there it is, the man in me, the Michigan in me, the villain with a gun in me, I suppose. A satisfaction in that action, to be unseen, to open someone from five hundred yards in slow-mo and watch the action happen through your scope, I mean in games I am playing games I mean it's me I'm doing it, I take an action and something happens and keeps happening and all I can see is from a distance like an epic simile I don't want to minimize me but there I am and you are too, we are a we together watching. Something's hatching all this time.

I SHOULD EXPLAIN A LITTLE BIT: I don't mean to be the subject here, but I do mean to be an instrument. I am a thing on which an effect is registered: one of many other things. I grew up in Michigan's remote Upper Peninsula, but I haven't lived there in many years. I had a good enough childhood—trees and fields and collapsed barns and dogs and snow and snow and snow—until my mother died when I was seven. After that I disappeared a bit in games or in the woods. Sometimes I would disappear in snow. My dad remarried shortly thereafter, and I wish I could say it was happily. What is happiness to a kid? I wonder now: My brother and I had friends. We did well in school. We read a ton. Blew some stuff up. Messed around in the woods. Nobody fell into an abandoned mine or died in snow, at least not anyone we knew well. It snowed more. We missed our mom but didn't talk about her often. My dad and my stepmother did not get along well, especially when he drank and she got mean. I remember running pretty wild then with my brother and our friends. There were punishments. For some reason I remember my parents hoarding beans, like bags and bags and bags of beans in the basement of our duplex, like we might need those beans when the bombs started dropping. It was right around when *Red Dawn* came out, a survivalist bootstrap fantasy of fighting in the woods and killing commies and shooting many, many RPGs (rocket-propelled grenades, for some reason the height of military tech in 1980s movies). The commies did not, in fact, attack. I played World War II games on the family PC. My parents divorced. With my dad, we moved. We got into older and bigger kinds of trouble, finding stashes of porn and messing around with bikes. We blew up bigger things. Shot guns, made weapons with our friends. Started getting into bombs. It snowed some more. It seemed to never stop snowing. I got into electronic bulletin boards and software piracy. My dad and stepmother started seeing each other again, much to my brother's and my displeasure. We all moved back in, I guess. A few years later, we moved to Saudi Arabia. My stepmother moved with us to Riyadh for a while. I got way deeper into computer networks from afar, started hacking and taking up phone phreaking. I got sent away to boarding school for academic reasons. My brother stayed in the Middle East. The United States attacked Iraq.

BACK ON-SCREEN NOW, we get a helicopter, pretty much the exact same kind we'd send in to Iraq in the first Operation Desert Storm. "Carl Weathers. Elpidia Carrillo"—the sole female actor in the movie. Then multiple helicopters. The music's martial. It makes me want to march. We don't yet know where we are or what we're doing here or what kind of movie this is, exactly, but it's definitely hot. Everyone is sweating. Here's a military guy. Then Carl Weathers in a white shirt with a not-great tie, glistening. This is the movie that—to me—defined him, though he had already become famous for playing Apollo Creed in the *Rocky* movies. He's been good in lots of other stuff since. A fan circulates air on the screen.

In the living room in 2021 I sit underneath the ceiling fan. Neither my wife nor my daughter likes sitting underneath, but I can't get enough of it, especially in the summer in Tucson, where it's 111 degrees outside and, as a fairly big dude, I chafe and sweat. Back to the chopper where we see the team that we'll follow into the jungle, all a bunch of big dudes. Not regular big but *really* big, particularly Blain—played by Jesse Ventura—in an MTV T-shirt. Billy, Mac. Some other guys. At least one guy I only noticed on this viewing getting off the helicopter whom we'll never see again in the movie. I don't know who he is. They're all in casual clothes. Once they get out we finally see Schwarzenegger, still in the helicopter, lighting a cigar. He gets out too. A shot of some folks on a beach watching this disembarking take place. Three brown kids on the right of the screen stare right at the camera: they're staring at the guys, as you do if a bunch of helicopters land a couple of hundred feet away from you and hulking American dudes get out. The kids look maybe a year or two younger than I was when I watched the movie for the first time.

I'M NOT SURE HOW MY OBSESSION with *Predator* started. I first watched it in 1987 or maybe the year after. I was twelve, so no way was I able to see it on the big screen. If I did see it in a theater, I don't remember it, but I do remember a family friend taking me and my brother to see *Revenge of the Nerds* (rated R) a couple of years earlier, which had way less violence but a lot more nudity. That was my introduction to the world of films made for adults: jokes about beer and bush and race and sexual orientation and panty raids. I'm not sure, in retrospect, if *Predator* was made for adults, even if I love it as an adult. It definitely feels like it was made for teens. Tweens even. It's that big and cartoonish, violent and comic, in fact, a kind of violent comic, aimed right at the pleasure centers of teenagers with a healthy disconnect between cause and effect. But if I saw *Revenge of the Nerds* on the big screen I could have seen *Predator* there, too, likely at the Lode Theater in downtown Houghton. It was called the Lode because Houghton was a copper-mining town, set among dozens of other copper-mining towns, though the mines had closed down well before I was born, and really all we had was the memory of those mines, the stories of those mines and those who worked them, the run that this place had, that flush of money, now long gone, and all we had growing up was a bunch of holes in the ground that you weren't supposed to go in but of course you did, and mine tailings down by the lake and other lakes with cancerous fish you were definitely not supposed to eat. If I didn't see it at the Lode, I guess it might have been at the Pic, the competing theater in Hancock, the competing town across the Portage Canal. Or, way more likely, I may have seen *Predator* first on VHS or Betamax a year later at a friend's house after we got someone's older brother to rent it for us from Very Video.

These days there are lots of other predators for us to consider aside from the one in the movie. The most obvious are the unmanned drones that America relies on in our interventions in foreign countries. Pilots fly them remotely as if playing video games not that far off the games I used to play myself, except with incredible graphics and actual effects. These are increasingly disturbing agents of war, though they also feature domestically, as they're deployed to police and surveil our borders. Recently— disturbingly—we saw them in the skies above Minneapolis's protests over the death of George Floyd. Now that we've largely cleared our country of apex predators like jaguar and cougar, we find that we live in a land of human predators: sexual predators, mass shooters, serial killers, nearly all of them men. One of those men killed my friend's sister in high school: we'll come back to that. These are not purely abstract ideas. I have vivid memories of my friends and myself planning some kind of insurrection in the town, probably after watching *Red Dawn*, figuring out which buildings we'd have to take, and with what weaponry. Would we take the radio station first, or would we have to take out the power plant down by the water? It was a joke, of course, and it was also not a joke. I mean, we thought both things is what I mean. The line between our reality and our fantasy was not at all as thick as it became later as adults (for most of us, at least). In these plans we felt like we had power. I don't regret these feelings.

In the weeks after the Safeway shooting in Tucson, I found myself playing first-person shooter games, most obviously *Fallout 3*, in which I'd use a sniper rifle to shoot marauders in the head. When I got a particularly good shot off, the game showed me the shot and then the marauders' heads exploding in slow motion. It's a thrilling and dramatic effect, combining the slow-motion replay of sports with the violent fetish of action movies and wrapping it all in a game mechanic, so it's *me* doing the thing that I'm seeing in slow motion. It's impossible not to love. Or I love it anyway. Yes, this practice was an increasingly jarring form of self-care, I realized, but I found—and still find—it deeply satisfying. There's a reason why people play so many first-person shooter games. Part of the appeal for me then was pulling back some sense of control from my environment in which even something as banal as a Safeway was no longer safe.

What was even more jarring was that in *Fallout 3* you wander around the ruins of a postapocalyptic Washington, DC, one ripped, as *Law and Order* says, from the headlines. Here's the Washington Monument, of course. Here's the White House. Here are the subways that you crawl through, shooting various things, on your way from one area to another. I don't think I'd actually *been* to Washington, DC, or not to the famous parts of it, until after I'd played the game. Walking down not-yet-totally-collapsed roads into some of the very same scenes I'd already played was shockingly weird, an odd elision of my experience in a game and an experience I was having live. And this was way before the morons stormed the Capitol at the end of the Trump era, which is a thing you can also do in *Fallout 3*, though in the game's defense, it's postapocalypse, it's not as if we have a functioning government or even running water, and it is literally kill or be killed as mutants, irradiated creeps, and various bands of bad actors roam the land.

In the game I was the one doing the shooting: I was the protagonist.

Through my early twenties, I spent a good bit of my life creating problems for others (especially my dad and stepmother). Committing a healthy bit of vandalism, some shoplifting, some negligence with fire and fireworks and weaponry, and later making bombs and breaking into Michigan Bell trucks and dorm rooms and (electronically) banks and credit bureaus and so forth and so on, getting kicked out of high school and arrested and convicted, and later incurring the wrath (again) of the Secret Service and doing more garden-variety sorts of insurrections against the tyrannies of the adult world. Having spent much of my life creating problems for others (especially my dad and stepmother), I think of myself these days as someone who tries to solve them, at least some of the time, even if it's just in games.

After I'd shot who knows how many mutants and random brigands and actual time had passed in our actual world in which my congresswoman had been actually shot, the news said Giffords was stabilized and then released from the hospital and back into her own life and also to some extent into ours. Then I also found myself rewatching *Predator*. I finished it, and turned it back on again.

THE MOVIE HASN'T LEFT US the way you'd think, like others of its ilk (*Commando*, for instance, or *Raw Deal*). *Predator* is a movie about both the future and the past. It's a sci-fi movie wrapped in a horror movie wrapped in a war movie wrapped in a space movie. It's satire wrapped in gun pornography. It's tenderness wrapped in beefy macho posturing and explosive ballets.

In fact, it started as a joke. Since Rocky kept kicking the ass of everyone in the late '70s and early '80s, including the seemingly invulnerable Ivan Drago of *Rocky IV*, it seemed clearly nothing earthly was left for Rocky to fight. Thus the next one, some folks joked, would have to be *Rocky vs. E.T.*

It's a bad idea, but like many bad ideas, it was a seed that stuck around. That seed became a script, written by brothers Jim and John Thomas, and finally Schwarzenegger got attached to it, and *Predator* got made, and while in some ways the movie is still a joke (it *is* ridiculous, like, way over the top with some of its bits, and it is full of jokes), it's not *just* a joke. It's about men and the way they relate to us, to themselves, and to each other more spectacularly than any other film I can think of, particularly any other film with a shitload of guns and an alien.

I mean: It's a dumb movie. It's a big dumb movie. But it's not *just* a big dumb movie. Two of its stars later became US governors: first Jesse Ventura in Minnesota, then Arnold Schwarzenegger in California. That makes it have to mean something. American politics ate our big dumb movie and our big dumb guys. It's not that hard to draw a line from *Predator* to pro wrestlers' and body builders' becoming governors and now our whole culture's becoming more and more like a big dumb movie. And this is a *fun* big dumb movie, one that I and lots of people like me all ate whole, over and over, in the '80s and in the '90s, and we keep on eating it.

LAST NIGHT MY WIFE and I watched an hourlong compilation of the best action-movie trailers of the 1980s, and, watching all of them back-to-back-to-back, their similarities were apparent. I was usually able to identify the movie within the first five seconds of each trailer, a trick I imagine Megan became rapidly tired of. The exception was trying to differentiate some of the Steven Seagal movies from one another; my accuracy with those movies went down to about 70 percent. But for everything else I was batting 1.000. By the time we finished the series of trailers, I realized I had seen them *all*, even the terrible ones, or the ones that seemed meaningful at the time but now bleed into one another and disappear into landfills of decaying VHS tapes. Inexplicably, this montage of trailers omitted everything by Jean-Claude Van Damme except for the movie where he and Dolph Lundgren share top billing: *Universal Soldier*. Perhaps this was because they featured fewer guns? I've seen all of Van Damme's movies also, of course. Who hasn't? And the *Lethal Weapon* movies were also nowhere to be found. Check, check, check. I wondered: How many American action movies had I *not* seen during this period? Had I missed *any* at all? I did some digging and made a list of those I watched between 1985 and 1995:

Above the Law, Action Jackson, Aliens, Big Trouble in Little China, Blood Sport, Cliffhanger, Cobra, Code of Silence, Commando, Conan the Barbarian, Conan the Destroyer, The Crow, Cyborg, The Dead Pool, Death Warrant, Death Wish, Death Wish 2, Death Wish 3, The Delta Force, The Delta Force 2, Demolition Man, Die Hard, Die Hard 2, Die Hard with a Vengeance, Double Impact, Escape from New York, Executive Decision, Extreme Prejudice, First Blood, Hard Target, Hard to Kill, Heartbreak Ridge, Hudson Hawk, Invasion USA, Iron Eagle, Iron Eagle II, Judge Dredd, Kickboxer, Judgment Night, Last Action Hero, The Last Boy Scout, Lethal Weapon, Lethal Weapon 2, Lethal Weapon 3, Lionheart, Lock Up, Mad Max, Mad Max 2: the Road Warrior, Mad Max: Beyond Thunderdome, Marked for Death, Missing in Action, Missing in Action 2, On Deadly Ground, Out for Justice, Over the Top, Passenger 57, Point Break, Predator, Predator 2, The Punisher, Rambo: First Blood Part II, Rambo III, Raw Deal, Red Dawn, Red Heat, Red Scorpion, Red Sonja, Ricochet, Robocop, The Running Man, Street Fighter, Sudden Death, Tango & Cash, The Terminator, Terminator 2, Timecop, Total Recall, True Lies, Under Siege, Under Siege 2, Universal Soldier.

Later, I would watch many more. I didn't include *Road House*, because when I watched it with my wife last year I had seemingly no memory of it. It surprised me that I wouldn't have seen it then, but don't worry: I have now. I wasn't sure what to make of it, in fact: it starts out as kind of a fun fighting and preening movie with Hot Guy Patrick Swayze, but by its end it becomes a surprisingly brutal action movie, guns and shootouts and all. At any rate, the list above comprises approximately one week of continuous action movie viewing, if you didn't stop and never slept. I can't even count the number of explosions, bullets fired, one-liners, sound effects of fists hitting flesh, Wilhelm screams, bursts of blood, extremities broken or cut off by blades or guns or bombs, or the total body count.

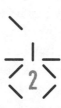

You're Looking Good, Dutch

BACK ON-SCREEN IN *PREDATOR*, here's a body, if one of the less important ones in the movie. It's General Phillips, who's essential only for the next few minutes. He comments on Schwarzenegger as he enters, "You're looking good, Dutch."

Which is true: he is. No one talks enough about how Schwarzenegger looks on-screen. Or how his face is lit in every shot: That jaw! Those eyes! His perfect skin! I can see why California made him governor. In 1987 I would have appointed him chief deity; he's as close as we were going to get to it on the human side of the dividing line, at least that year. Since, his star has waned, as they do. It's good they do. Because he'll die eventually, he's more beautiful than something cast in bronze. I try to explain this principle to my daughter without success. Age becomes a thing he plays, I say: the old machine in *Terminator 2*. The older machine in *Terminator 3*. The yet older machine in *Terminator: Genisys*. These things keep rebooting: 2019's *Terminator: Dark Fate* also features Schwarzenegger playing an even older machine (though—spoiler—he finally dies, to the degree that a machine can die—at the end). He plays the retro action hero (among other older models) in throwback ensemble *The Expendables 1, 2,* and *3.* Machines get old. Men do too.

It pleases us to love an older model in the age of the new. Look at the way that in a world of digital plenty we fetishize the object: vinyl and tape and VHS. We watch and we remember the days before cell phones and connectivity and CGI and how our dreams were delivered then. We can crack open the shells of who we used to be if we can access the technology. We are still in there. It only takes a movie or a game to unlock us. I know I'm just a fetishist like you for it.

The film caricatures itself: these men are big. They always have been, it seems, and in memory they will stay that way. Schwarzenegger was nearly forty at the time of filming. Nearly all of the actors are still alive—except for Sonny Landham (Billy) and Kevin Peter Hall, the man inside the Predator suit. We'll get to him in a little while. You never get to see Hall's face except in an uncredited cameo at the end, on the chopper. A few years later, he died of complications due to HIV, allegedly the result of a blood transfusion. It's possible that story's even true. Nothing reliable I've found suggests otherwise, even if he did play the monster in the closet in *The Monster in the Closet.* It's tempting to extrapolate from that fact.

The Predator itself—we'll see him soon enough, but for now it's a title and a name—is unknowable. To call it a beast is false. It is a thing, a being. A monster: sure. Monster means what we're afraid of. It thinks. It stinks. It can't sing but it has a code.

Action films are great, because action is a great short-term response to grief. Your mom died? Go blow something up! Split some wood! Craft some traps. Shoot a giant gun into the trees. Set something on fire, intentionally or unintentionally: either way, it burns. That is, when you move it gives no space to feeling. It's fine for the long term too: like us, action movies will never sag or slow and touch the ground. Keep moving and creating and you'll never feel what hit you long ago. As Blain, Jesse Ventura's character, says, famously, you "ain't got time to bleed." Which is true. Until you do, and then you know.

Ventura is a kind of father. Ditto Schwarzenegger. Sex symbol, sure. Icon: totally. Signpost: yes. They're not playing characters: they play themselves, or whatever there is of themselves, these men always performing. That's heroism. None of the characters in the film were fathers, though they talk a lot about pussy. That's how twelve-year-olds imagine men talk. Some men—some presidents even—do talk this way, maybe having learned it from films like this. None of the characters has a relationship with a woman, nor with any characters outside the screen. Nothing indicates any of these men has even ever met an adult woman until they take one prisoner partway through.

INSIDE, GENERAL PHILLIPS is still explaining some stuff that's not important. We don't have to pay attention to everything. The camera shows us maps. Their territories are unidentifiable, or if they could be identified, I couldn't tell you where we are. What country it is. *Predator* was filmed in Mexico, and it's supposed to be set in an unnamed Central American country. The most recent major conflict on most Americans' minds was in Vietnam, though America had been intervening covertly in Central and South America and many other countries for much of the last century. As the movie was being filmed, President Reagan bombed Libya, one of the screenwriters remembers: "It's a disconcerting feeling to be stuck down there in a foreign country and you have no idea what's going on." Except, producer Joel Silver reminded them, "We've got the guns. We've got millions in the bank. We can take over." Cinematographer Donald Alpine, in the same oral history of *Predator*, added, "Endlessly our director would defer to Joel about how much blood there would be, how gruesome should we make this? And Joel's answer was always 'more blood!'"

Well, we're a long way yet from that *more blood*. First we have to meet the bodies that hold the blood. In a grassy hut, the friends meet for the first time: Dutch and Dillon. They *are* friends, right? I think they're friends. Dutch says to Dillon, by way of greeting, "You son of a bitch," but with a smile, leading to one of many highly iconic (to boys like me, meaning mostly white and country to various degrees, the kind of boys we were then in Michigan, the kind of men we would later become outside Michigan) scenes in this movie, scenes that continue to echo and echo through my life. The big white guy (Dutch) and the big Black guy (Dillon) clasp arms in what is halfway between a hug and a handshake. It's clearly a familiar greeting for these two, but it turns into a test of strength as they each try to overpower the other. This is how I understood men to behave when they encountered other men.

In the July 27, 1985, version of the script, then titled *Hunter*, a couple of drafts before the shooting script, these two men are strangers, which would make for a very different movie. In that script they've never met. There's no manful test of strength. They don't even touch or look meaningfully into each other's eyes. Dillon "extends his hand, a cold smile on his face." Dutch turns, disregarding his hand. That's it. But in the January 30, 1987, version of the script, the draft that's closest to the shooting script, "the two men step forward and simultaneous[ly] swing from the hip as if to land a punch . . . but their hands SLAP together in a gesture of friendship, their forearms bulging, testing each other's strength." This is pretty close to what we see on-screen. These, we're given to understand, are Men with a capital *m*. The SLAP is all caps! They're as BIG as they COME. Dominant. Tough. Military. Not to be FUCKED WITH. They will be outfitted with the biggest, coolest GUNS one can find, so big, in fact, that one had to be invented for the movie. They're American, of course, because heroes always are.

AS MEN, WHAT THEY SAY—and they don't say a lot—is not always what they mean. I should say: what *they* say, but also what *we* say. I am a man. At forty-five now, I'm only a few years older than

Schwarzenegger was when this film came out, though, full disclosure, I look a whole lot worse than he does here, having never done a crunch or a bicep curl (I didn't even know the term for this: I had to look it up, which should tell you something about my softness). Schwarzenegger is two years younger than my dad, a fact I didn't really think about as I watched and rewatched this movie for years, letting it parent me.

I mean, I know I'm watching *Predator* to watch myself: another reason we turn to art instead, we hope, of the internet, which holds our secrets poorly. M. H. Abrams hands us the metaphor well oiled: *Predator*'s a mirror or a lamp; possibly it's a projection booth. As we know, a film's not truth: what we see is light moving across a screen. It moves across everything, across all of us all the time. Besides, those metaphors have since been retired, like all technologies eventually: Now we have apps for that, the mirror and the lamp, and isn't a projection booth where Freud told you to go to see your troubles in another?

I was twelve the year *Predator* came out. What felt like a year later but Google says was five, Jodi Watts, my friend's sister and my former babysitter, was raped and murdered in a parking garage down the street from the Lode Theater, a garage where I used to hang out sometimes, right next to the Subway where many of us would gather and buy our shitty sandwiches. I don't have that many memories of Jodi now, but I do remember her calling me a fruitcake, fondly, as I was trying to rock myself to sleep too intensely and probably making a racket.

My friend loved guns before, but after that he started collecting them obsessively. I don't blame him. In my small way I was ruined too: I can't really get my head around what it would have been like for him, how hot he burned and for how long. He still burns, I'm sure. The whole city burns. I mean, this was not a town where people were murdered. Before this people didn't lock their doors. Now they did, and stared out their latched windows into the snowy night.

This is how we start to feel a story differently. I don't know that this story belongs here, but it's hard not to feel it bleed across my teenage years and my time with guns and camouflage and the place that grew me and hurt me, as Auden said "Mad Ireland" did Yeats, into poetry. There was not much light then in Michigan: January's a nearly lightless month of snow, and what sun can penetrate plays its film across the banks and frozen roads of the long dark about to come. It's actually the direct opposite of where I write this from: The Tucson summer, in which light is insane and unavoidable. It flattens us. Beats everything down. It fades the paint on houses. It melts CD cases and vinyl left in cars. You can—quite literally—bake cookies on the dashboard of your car (it takes several hours, and they don't brown, but they bake fine). When the sun goes down a weight lifts a little, even if the heat takes hours to dissipate. At night the temperature falls to maybe 80, then it all repeats. And here I am still watching *Predator* on the couch underneath the fan.

Did I watch the film with my friend? Probably, I'd bet: We watched it a lot those days, or maybe it was only me. And then we'd go to shoot at something after. Or maybe we both watched *Predator* on our own screens, burning in our own ways.

PREDATOR KEEPS MATTERING because its sci-fi fantasies are now the news. And the kind of large American manhood that the movie represents so gloriously has begun to seem to me increasingly sinister too. I see a guy walking down a street downtown with an AR-15 strapped to his back. Arizona doesn't require concealed carry permits for guns. And besides, that guy isn't concealing anything. Or, like all of us, he's concealing something—some soft part of us underneath all the weaponry and tech—even if it's hard to see it through his gun and the pose he strikes.

Walking through my suburban neighborhood I see a hand-lettered sign on a porch that reads "A heavily armed asshole lives here," alongside four SUVs adorned with gun stickers and each with the same window decal: "If I'm passing you on the right, you're the asshole." Not all of my neighbors in Tucson are so aggro, but enough of them are to make me a little nervous. This weaponed-up posture reminds me of home, but filtered through some half-assed mythology of the American West, though I suppose the reverse could be true. What used to be fringe is now everywhere.

Another neighbor flew a drone around our neighborhood every night last summer. I came to like and look forward to its unearthly light and buzz, taking my daughter on a walk and hearing it hovering somewhere above us like an insect or an alien, flashing its lights in the sky, making her shriek with glee. What *was* that flying thing anyway? Here, I wanted to tell her, was some neighborhood magic.

Then one day it disappeared. I asked a dude we walked by in the neighborhood about it a couple of days later. He said someone shot it, or tried to shoot it; either way, it definitely had it coming. It wasn't coming back. He fucking hated that thing. He thought it was an invasion of privacy. He thought it was creeping on him and his family in the backyard. He got noticeably redder the longer he monologized about this. After that the owner posted signs asking about its whereabouts and offering a reward, but I never saw the drone again. I can see both positions, but mostly I was sad to see it go.

I never thought to ask the guy who owned the drone if he ever found out what happened to it. He drove a 2015 Dodge Challenger, orange and meaty and aggressive with a racing stripe along the side. The Challenger is the only muscle car I'm drawn to as an adult for reasons I can't articulate. I've never gone for Mustangs: they're obvious and dull. They're meathead cars, like the kind the assholes in high school used to drive or want to drive or talk about driving that most of the rest of us disregarded. No one drives Trans-Ams anymore, so they no longer show up in my days (though they do occasionally populate my dreams). I still see a few Camaros, but they do not tempt me. No one I knew as a kid had a Challenger; they were—then—too old. They were primarily manufactured from 1970 to 1974, so by the late '80s nobody would have driven them, or if they did, I don't remember. I've never even owned an American car. The rebooted Challenger has a frankly sexual appeal: it's big and wide, all muscle, sleek and gleaming, no time to bleed. My pulse jumps thinking about it, embarrassingly. When my friend Heidi told me her ex-husband bought one, I understood why immediately. While I wouldn't personally buy a Dodge (I have memories of one too many unreliable Dodges in our family), their whole redesigned, retro, muscly line (the Charger! the Challenger! even the Dart!) sings to me every time I see one, like the Predator.

SO SINCE I'M HERE WATCHING *Predator* again tonight for viewing number 146, I realize this fact probably puts me in the company of a very elite squad of obsessive nerds. Surely a lot of us have guns. Probably all of us play video games in which we have guns and blow shit up. When I ask a new friend if he plays games, not wanting to assume (I do have friends who do not play games), he stares at me as if I'm nuts and says, "I'm a guy in his late thirties. Of course I fucking play games!" Some of us—like my childhood friend Graham—actually have guns and blow shit up for their jobs. In real life (meatspace, as we used to say in the early days of online), some of us dress up in our homemade Predator suits. A couple of years ago, some of us tried to buy an elaborate homemade Predator suit from a guy in Phoenix we met on Craigslist for $1,000, only to be turned away because we were insufficiently serious and almost certainly too fat. Perhaps that guy did not mean to sell his suit at all, but wanted to find a friend.

This year, 2021, is not a great time to find friends. I'm at home. I'm social distancing. It's a pandemic, speaking of invisible predators. It's summer in Tucson. It's hot as hell, 111 today, well above 100 most days with clouds or drones a rare reprieve. Mount Lemmon, where we try to escape from the summer heat, is burning (125,000 acres burned as of this writing), so no one's allowed up there. It smokes and smolders, lines of fire crisscrossing it. You can see it at night. It looks like Mordor. We stay inside unless we can't anymore, but it's not as if there are that many places to go, with the bars and restaurants and even the movie theaters closed. We're trying to stay alive here. We have no time to bleed. We're trying to be part of a community, to do something for us. We wear our masks. We give money to bail funds for protestors arrested both here and in Minneapolis and in other cities. By we I mean I, but I also mean we, or I hope I mean we.

Watching *Predator* is being part of something else, a synecdoche. I don't always like the something else that it is. It's big and stupid and a spectacle. It's the '80s, so it's at least a little racist and sexist and homophobic in some measure. America was trying to prove something to itself then. America is always telling stories to itself. But it's also beautiful, this film, this place, these men, and what the action will soon bring out of them. "She would of been a good woman," the Misfit says in Flannery O'Connor's "A Good Man Is Hard to Find," "if it had been somebody there to shoot her every minute of her life."

It's also true, though, that *Predator* isn't what you think it will be going into it. Or, more accurately, it's what you think it is, but it's *also* several something elses. It's an action movie gone awry. It's big masculinity. Big weaponry. Big American hubris. It also intends to undermine these things, which is one reason why it still speaks to me. It's less white than you'd think. And of all those big dumb action movies of the '80s, this is the one that's stayed with us the longest, spawning three direct sequels and a couple of crossover *Alien vs. Predator* movies, not even to get into the games and the comics and the action figures.

A Simple Setup

SO HERE'S THE DEAL. "Simple setup: one day operation. We pick up their trail at the chopper, run them down, grab those hostages, and get back across the border before anybody knows we're there."

Another close-up of the map. "Code 4096" at 23:22. I love this detail! I have no idea how accurate this is, what "Code 4096" means, if anything. Likely nothing: it's got the *feel* of information, but feel is all there probably is. The C130 penciled in may refer to the Air Force transport planes, the kind that are stationed down at the Davis-Monthan Air Force Base six miles away from my house.

Tucson is the home of the 309th Aerospace Maintenance and Regeneration Group (AMARG), better known as the Boneyard, a place where military aircraft come to die, and occasionally to be cannibalized or reborn. The website tells me it's the "sole . . . reclamation facility for all excess military and government aircraft."

I've run now a couple of Boneyard 10ks on the base, huffing through the long rows of gleaming planes. Running this race is one of the only ways short of a direct invitation to get on base and among the aircraft, and seeing all these planes in person that I've only seen in movies or games or books gives me a sense of scale:

oh shit, here are the *actual* machines of war. Theoretically, you can schedule a tour way in advance, but if they do a security check to get on base, I'm not 100 percent sure I'd pass it. As I mentioned before, some of the trouble I got into caught up with me at seventeen, and after a Secret Service Electronic Crime Task Force raided my boarding school dorm room while I was away on vacation, I ended up convicted of seven felonies for computer and telephony crimes. This was as a juvenile, so theoretically these records are all sealed, but you know how much secrets like to stay secret, and besides, all I got was probation and a lot of community service hours during which I was instructed to help people "use computers for good" (according to the judge) and a couple of years when my life was totally rerouted. I was forcibly removed from the culture I had spent so much time in and completely lost touch with the computer-hacking and phreaking communities I once identified so strongly with. This wasn't the end of my life interfacing with machines (I'm interfacing with a machine as I type this very sentence and I take *such* pleasure in this, the processing of words, the way all I have to do is stroke the keys and—*boom*—the words appear on the simulated page!), and I remain very interested in systems and reusing and repurposing them. All of this is to say that, combined with that little joke spoofing a friend's email account to threaten the life of the president (it was a *joke*: if I'd been serious, you would have never caught me) that earned me another visit from the Secret Service, I'm confident I do indeed have a record. Is that enough to keep me off the base? To make me a threat? I am, after all, a white guy. I'm not from money, but I didn't grow up poor. That carries a lot of weight and privilege in this world. In any case I sign up for the runs. I like to run among the machines. It's a crazy feeling, running—being a body—among literally a trillion dollars worth of (largely excess) military might. Mostly that might is in various states of disrepair, big tarps covering parts of the planes, but the impression I can't help but have is that of a sleeping giant. I would not want to fuck with this. This is probably the point.

Davis-Monthan is one of the three biggest employers here in Tucson, along with the University of Arizona, where I work, and Raytheon, who makes missile guidance systems and all kinds of highly classified tech and is one of the biggest makers of war machines the world has ever seen. No one who works there is allowed to talk about it. (Raytheon did also accidentally invent the microwave I use to warm my coffee in the afternoon: an oddity.)

I mean that my new city is built on the threat (or countering the threat) of war. On a tour of one of the former MX nuclear missile silos in Sahuarita, a forty-five-minute drive from my home, I see a map with a dozen missile sites in a ring around Tucson. It is a jarring reminder of how close we felt, growing up in the 1980s, to total nuclear war. The tour guides who take us down into the silo used to be stationed here, back then. They were the ones who had the matching keys that, when turned, launched a missile with a warhead. I get to sit in one of the two chairs playing the role of the pair of guys who would launch nuclear missiles by turning keys in tandem, like in the movies. Above the key lock, there is a dial with an *A*, a *B*, and a *C* on it. I ask the guide, "What does that refer to?" "Those were the targets," he says. "There were always three. Go ahead and switch it to *C*," he says. I do. "I'll count to three, and you and your partner turn the key," he says. I look at my partner, a twelve-year-old kid. We lock eyes when we reach three. We turn the key. "Boom," he says. "If that was live," the tour guide says, "you'd have sent a missile toward its target and killed millions, probably. Billions, maybe, once you factored in echoing, escalating responses."

"Did you know what the targets were?" I ask. He says they were never told—for the obvious reason that very few people would ever turn the key if they knew what and where and who they were striking.

Some Bad Things Happened in My Past

MY FRIEND'S SISTER was raped and murdered, as I told you. Another friend, J, blew off his hand and nearly castrated himself with a homemade bomb. His father would later hang himself off the side of a water tower for reasons I never understood and assume were unrelated. My mother died of cancer. A friend's mother, facing a terminal diagnosis, died by suicide. A second cousin electrocuted himself on a roof. Everyone knew someone who went through the ice on a snowmobile, which was a yearly occurrence in the town where I grew up. I nearly burned down my parents' farm trying to fire off model rockets in the field. My father turned his energies and all his angers to drinking. R's sister's fiancé died in a plane crash downstate. B and his friends guillotined and electrocuted chipmunks. They got into vandalism. I got into vandalism. Some of us got arrested for vandalism. We got into shoplifting. We blew stuff up with whatever we could find or make. We read *The Anarchist Cookbook*. A neighbor's kid blew half his face off in a suicide attempt. A few years later he completed the job. We all got into Dungeons & Dragons. I got deeper into shoplifting. B got into shoplifting. B and I got into more vandalism. M got into vandalism. I got into computers. G and I got into playing military flight simulator video games. I moved to Saudi Arabia. Got sent off to an American school where, armed with pepper spray and smoke bombs, G and I broke into Michigan Bell trucks and stole telephone gear and anything else we could find. I got into hacking. G got into hacking and phone phreaking. I got into credit card fraud. J got into credit card fraud. I hacked into credit bureaus. I started a bulletin board system (BBS) called, unsubtly, Datacrime International. I called myself, equally unsubtly, the Grim Reaper. A Secret Service task force raided my room at boarding school. I hacked into Comerica Bank and got questioned by the cops and some IT guys from the bank. Thereafter I was forbidden to have a telephone in my room, so I wired one illegally from the junction box. I rewired the pay phone in the lobby to one of the professor's phones so we could all call international for free. I stole a set of master keys, rewired the phones, and secretly rerouted one to my friend J's room, where we set up an illegal BBS inside a dresser with a false front. I stole a television from a porno theater in Cyprus. I got caught. M got into pot. D got into pot. D got into psychedelics and the Stone Roses. G got into pot, then cocaine, then crack, then cat, then meth. As far as I know he never got into heroin. I started to get away from him. A got into drinking. M got into white supremacy. J got arrested for credit card fraud ordering pizzas for delivery to his home using a credit card belonging to Bill Clinton that I had given him. J ended up narcing me out, and I got expelled from school. I got those seven felony convictions. K got into Amway. I got into Satanism. We all got into grunge. I got into goth. I got into industrial. Driving with J in my parents' borrowed car I hit a gas pump with the car and fled the scene. J's parents got divorced. My dad got remarried. My dad got divorced. My dad got remarried to the same person—this time without telling me or my brother (we found out after, by letter). I was questioned by the Secret Service for making death threats against the president as a joke and spoofing emails.

I got back into shoplifting. I got a job. The Michigan Militia guy I worked with at Walmart tried to recruit me unsuccessfully. The recruiting videos he had me watch were not compelling. I got out of shoplifting. We blew up tons of stuff. We had a lot of fun. I quit before I was fired.

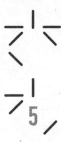

Gonna Have Me Some Fun Tonight

WE'RE SLOWLY MOVING CLOSER to the main story now, as we cut to the choppers flying low over the treetops. As we're about to be properly introduced to the team, we hear Little Richard's "Long Tall Sally" playing. Where's it coming from? We're not conditioned to ask, this being a movie. Often there are songs. Yet this will be the only recognizable song in the entire film. The rest of its soundtrack is sound effects and the original score. When I first watched the movie I paid the song little attention, though it sets the tone well enough, with its chorus of "havin' me some fun tonight" ringing out as we're preparing to have some fun tonight. It's a fun rock song. This is a fun movie. This movie is, first, fun for us, if not necessarily for the characters, who are, as you'd imagine, coming in for more than they expected. Most of them will not make it back out of the jungle.

I'm reminded how pumped up I used to get from the pump-up song that my hockey coach put on before games: "The Final Countdown," by Europe. I don't remember if we requested it or if it was his choice, but like *Predator* and Mötley Crüe and the Dodge Challenger it still reliably kick-starts my heart. It's kind of a dumb song in the genre most popular at the time—hair metal—but unlike a lot of those songs, it was weirder than it seemed. It's a sci-fi anthem about leaving earth for (checks notes) Venus, sung as a half lament, half celebration, global in scope and vaguely referencing nuclear apocalypse. As I learned, it's irritating to sing as a karaoke song since the second half of the song is repeating "It's the final countdown" over and over in your best falsetto, to diminishing returns, as you start to question what that lyric even *is*. It gets rapidly denatured, very weird, increasingly desperate and hollow, even, as you sing it over and over again. Eventually you kind of want to stop, but you're so far into it by this point that you want to see where it ends. If it ends, exactly.

Little Richard recorded "Long Tall Sally" in 1956, thirty years before *Predator*. So why is *this* the one song we're hearing in the movie? The one song in the *entire* movie? And why *this* version? Alternate takes 1 and 6 (you can listen to these two on the deluxe edition of 1957's *Here's Little Richard*) are much slower than the album version. Take 1 is almost half-time and in another key. Take 6 is a little peppier. Take 5, not on that deluxe album, comes in between the two of them, and like take 6, it features a longer piano solo. Take 1 omits this, though the album version—the one you've heard—has a longer sax solo in its stead. When you hear the album version you understand why they picked it: it's much faster, way more propulsive. According to a 2020 *Rolling Stone* article, they kept pushing the tempo with each take to make it so fast that (white) Pat Boone (who had denatured—to greater commercial effect—[Black] Little Richard's songs before) wouldn't be able to keep up with it. Whatever the reason, the energy in the version they released—and the one in *Predator*—is off the charts. It's way more fun. It gives Little Richard more to do. And he did a lot.

Little Richard, who described himself as omnisexual, was certainly anything other than straight. He sometimes performed in drag, and was openly gay for much of his life even though he struggled to reconcile his sexuality with his religion, especially as he grew older. He seems like an odd choice to soundtrack a hyper-masculine action movie like *Predator*. But it's canny in that, like "Tutti Frutti," Little Richard's other massive early hit, "Long Tall Sally" contains a lot more than it may seem at first listen. Both contain coded drag references and celebrate something that, considered closely, looks a lot like something other than straight-up heterosexual sex. Long Tall Sally, while "built sweet" and having "everything that Uncle John need," sure seems to contain some secrets: "I saw Uncle John with bald-head Sally / He saw Aunt Mary comin' and he ducked back in the alley, oh, baby . . . havin' me some fun tonight." This line is followed by the song's sax solo, in which, if we weren't dancing our asses off, we might use to think about what the song seems to say and what other things it also says.

Sometimes you have to contain multitudes to say an unsayable thing. Poets know.

As it turns out, Pat Boone did take his version of the song to number 8 on the pop chart, as Joe Levy notes in "The Wild Heart of Rock & Roll," an outstanding retrospective of Little Richard published in *Rolling Stone* in 2020: "It is doubtful Boone understood that the baldheaded Sally being snuck through the alley was another of Richard's coded celebrations of drag. But again, Richard did, his musicians did, and the knowledge filled the world with a freedom song clear in its intent if not identity."

According to Charles White's authorized biography of Little Richard, Richard had always been an outsider, something other than the social norm: "The kids would call me faggot, sissy, freak, punk. They called me everything. . . . I *felt* like a girl. . . . I just felt I wanted to be a girl more than a boy. . . . If I ever went out to friends' houses on my own, the guys would try to catch me, about eight or twenty of them together. . . . They didn't like my action." There are lots of secrets in Little Richard's songs. Until I went down the rabbit hole, I had no idea, for instance, that his famous single "Tutti Frutti" was similarly coded. As he said in White's biography, "I couldn't talk back to the boss, so instead of saying bad words, I'd say 'wop bop a loo bop a lop bam boom,' so he didn't know what I was thinking." Levy points out that "the girls Richard name-checked [in "Tutti Frutti"]—Daisy and Sue—were coded drag references. Those outside the life that Richard lived might not hear them as such." But the musicians and the label knew.

I can't not think, writing this, of my deep love of the band Erasure (and others of the less-than-totally-straight-vanilla synth bands of the '80s and '90s) as a teenager. My brother did not approve, so he'd blast the Geto Boys, and I would respond by blasting Enya's "Orinoco Flow," and he became so enraged by Enya telling him to sail away, sail away, sail away that he threw my *Watermark* tape on the roof of our house. My playing of Erasure's *The Circus* tape on repeat (sample lyric: "One day the boy decided / to let them know the way he felt inside") in response to his Iron Maiden ("I am a Viking / and you will taste my steel") would make him apoplectic, which I found very funny.

I mean: most art and pop culture is a similar collision of intentions and histories, only some of which are legible to any individual reader/viewer. Anything that achieves a modicum of commercial success depends on a whole bunch of people with different agendas and histories helping to make, produce, record, perform, mix, promote, or distribute it. What people hear or see is only a slice of what the thing actually is, especially if it's any good at all, and so it's often the case where some wildly popular pop/art phenomena have subversive layers that are completely missed by many of its fans, and that's part of what I love about Little Richard, and it's definitely part of what I love about *Predator*.

Did Little Richard like *Predator*? Did he ever watch it? What did he make of it, if so? If he watched these greased-up guys sparring in the helicopter, would he have found it familiar? Appealing? Appalling? Hilarious? Toxic? Arousing?

For me, *Predator* is all of these things in some degree, and when I watch it, each time I see it a little differently, which is surely why I keep coming back to it.

To a 2021 sensibility this scene—and the whole movie really—reads more than a little homoerotic, or at least that's one of its layers. And the use of "Long Tall Sally" points to this tension at the heart of the film. I searched for "Long Tall Sally" on YouTube, and the top result is this chopper scene. For many viewers, the song and the scene are forever entwined, and if they start to think about its implications, things get uncomfortable quickly. The comments section on the video consists primarily of laments for the dead genius and the glorious movie and this scene in particular, people quoting *Predator* to each other, commenters who want to say something about the superiority of 1987's version of manhood and the subsequent wussification of American men, and those who gleefully point out the many homoerotic undertones of the movie and the song.

Little Richard died in 2020, so the most recent comments are split about half and half between talking about him and discussing masculinity. As this is the Internet, *discussing* may not be the best word. "Back in the days when Men were Men," lp700 says. Another commenter compares these guys to today's "beta cucks" and "hipsters" and "soy boys" and "snowflakes." Another makes a gay joke (there are a lot of gay jokes). AleisterMeowley (nice name) responds, suitably, "Yeah man that song by the flamboyantly gay rock star gets my testosterone heated up too big guy." To which, this legendary comeback by Hasan Genc, "You sound like a filthy ass beta male." Such is the world we have found ourselves in. Then a lacuna forms around various commenters calling each other gay, as if this was the '80s and we were still thirteen. Ward Luay pings in from the Middle East: "I was Always taught that girls need to be girls and men be manly and strong and protect the family." And then you get some combination of sincere comments and trolls, and I'm going to go ahead and sports metaphor my way out of this shithole. Maybe nuke it from orbit, honestly: that's the only way to be sure.

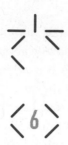

Fast-Forward: Billy,
Get Me a Way Out of This Hole

PREDATOR KNOWS this is a hole, and we need to find our way out. The film is a trap, but it's also *about* traps. There are a ton of them herein. To list a few: we'll see tripwires set by the guerrillas to catch our team, our team will make elaborate Boy Scout–style booby traps to catch the Predator, and Dutch himself will make yet more elaborate homemade traps to catch and kill the Predator. The Predator itself will lay traps to kill Dutch. And the whole situation the team finds itself in will be shown to be a trap of bad information and intentions. The way the team depends on all its guns and ordnance—a kind of stand-in for technological masculinity—also turns out to be a trap, in which these guys are caught. The shadow of the Vietnam War was a trap from which America has an incredibly difficult time extricating itself, to this day. So when halfway into the movie, Dutch instructs Billy to "find us a way out of this hole," I'm feeling the same way. We've come too far to turn back. And since here we are without backup, we'll need to find our own way out.

On book tour right before the 2020 pandemic hit, I had dinner with a couple of women in their twenties, and one of them asked

me: You write about men and masculinity. What do you think
is actually *good* or worth *saving* about masculinity? Is *anything*
good about masculinity? Or is it *over*?

I was taken aback not by the question but by its plainness. I was
also a little surprised to be asked so directly about masculinity, as
if I was an expert on it, but I do write about it, if at a slant. In retrospect, shouldn't I be an expert, being a male now for more than
forty years? I shouldn't have been surprised: as of 2021 men—
particularly the white, mostly straight men I grew up around—
have been digging our own hole for a while now. We keep being
assholes, if not predators. We keep fucking up politics. We keep
cheating and lying and groping and raping and feeling backed
into corners about our slightly reduced cultural domain. We're
feeling threatened and lashing out. It's hard for me to say *we* here,
since I feel like my Enya and Erasure tapes ought to disqualify
me from the dude crew, but I think it's important to own what—
indeed—I am. I'm implicating myself in this on account of being a
cis and (mostly) straight white man, which makes me—in the eyes
of my dining companions at least—part of the problem, or at least
someone who ought to be able to speak on behalf of men, who,
when we speak about this subject at all, are most often defensive
and angry and hostile. It's a bad pose, so maybe this is why they
were asking me, hoping for a better answer. But I have the same
questions for this we. I mean, I'm me, but it is a we I'm speaking
out of and a we I'm speaking toward.

I want to say I don't recognize myself in these guys. But I do,
if only at angles. I share almost all the same set of cultural references: action movies and hair metal and vandalism and misogyny:
check. How can I not be in some way the same? And, with the exception of the misogyny, I'm still down with action movies and
(some of) hair metal and (at a distance) the brute pleasures of vandalism. I destroyed a *lot* of shit as a teenager. A kid, really. I remember going down to the Ojibwe reservation to buy fireworks
around the Fourth of July every year: it was an open secret that

you could pretty much get whatever you wanted there, legal or not as it may have been off-reservation, and while my dad was probably there to pick up the cheap tobacco, I was there to buy things that smoked and flew and blew up. At six years old (I'm guessing now), I set off a couple of "Mammoth Smoke Bombs" in my bedroom in the farmhouse I grew up in because I was trying to smoke out a fly that had become trapped when I closed the window. I ended up burning the carpet in the room and remember the big scorch marks after, evidence of my asymmetric response. I don't know if I killed the fly.

I went on from there to use a lot of fireworks to blow up a lot of things, and that was before we got into *The Anarchist Cookbook* and the bombs and the guns, and here I am halfway to a Cranberries song without the political strife, which is a position I never expected to be in.

Still, in that moment at dinner, presented with that plain accusation about masculinity, I struggled to respond: What even *was* masculinity anyway? It seemed so basic and straightforward, but I had a hard time articulating it in a way that didn't feel awfully essentialist and reductive, and the more reductive it felt, the less appealing it sounded. I don't remember what I actually said, but I was thinking about the uses of aggression, competitiveness, assertion, some basic set of knowledges vaguely imparted by my father (who did teach me to do and make a number of things; he was— and is—also an excellent cook, the primary cook in our family, a skill I only embraced after my half-assed twenties of ramen and microwaved potatoes), or the things I believed my father should have taught me even if I learned them through reading ninja magazines and *Soldier of Fortune* and *Shotgun News* and watching *Predator*, or, more recently, YouTube videos and outdoor survival shows, and some combination of learned or innate drive. Is masculinity defensiveness? Is it being an asshole to everyone online? Is it not being able to take a joke or take a little bit of criticism and keep our shit together?

Is that it? Is that all? Maybe it's also leaning toward the glories of violence, too, all those hours of pleasurable and disturbing training? Is it that we're easily thrilled by explosions, like we were when we were kids? Is it a penchant for never shutting up? Put this way the package doesn't sound all that appealing, but then you light a fuse and HELL YEAH, it all comes back. There must be more to it than this. Invention, capability, ingenuity, play, a desire to solve problems, a desire to protect and to defend: these qualities feel relevant too. And they're certainly not restricted to "men."

I'm no biologist, but it's pretty obvious to me that more of this behavior is learned rather than innate. Or, at least in my case, I understand a lot of this is how I've been trained to feel. Still, this masculinity is not the kind I've always particularly identified with or felt particularly capable of or infused by. I'm asthmatic. I washed out of high school football on account of allergies to grass but also general wussiness and boredom. I'm easily intimidated by the jockeying of men, especially when in large groups. I like the intricacies of typography and like to discuss serifs. I stan the Pet Shop Boys. I have a lot of feelings about Sarah McLachlan pre-1993. Oh, I definitely went to Lilith Fair, if in the company of my girlfriend. I'm an okay listener. I fucking *golf.* Worse, I *disc golf.* Which is where I seem to hear a lot of *Predator* being quoted.

The downsides of masculinity, particularly when unchallenged and taken to extremes, are more and more obvious these days. Go online—like to those YouTube comments on Little Richard—and men reveal their uglinesses quickly: violence, ignorance, bullying, and other toxicities. But I also don't think it's something we can or even should eliminate either. Or I suppose if we did that puts me on the extinction list, so perhaps I can't contemplate it for this reason.

I DIDN'T FEEL *THREATENED* by this dinner conversation exactly, but I was definitely dismayed. This was the situation young women found themselves in when trying to meet someone interesting, or trying to have conversations with young men? They each had some pretty entertaining stories about the guys they'd tried to date recently in the city, possibly elaborated on for my sake. Listening, I felt depressed for men. For women too. For everybody really. I mean, it's not as if I was a peach to date in my twenties either. I rented a basement with an unfinished ceiling so that I'd be watching *Twin Peaks* with a potential girlfriend, and suddenly bats would be swooping down on us. I had a Spice Girls poster on my bedroom wall: also, you know, for the ladies. It was ironic but also not. My culinary skills consisted of microwaving baked potatoes, which I did early and often, and swamping them in sour cream. Needless to say, I drove a crappy car. At this time I was very into Hawaiian shirts. I was, however, mostly, probably, not an asshole, so there was that. I came to my own issues honestly, as most of us do. I was muddling through. At least I rarely lashed out at others.

All this thinking about masculinity started to tire me, so I took a break to go shoot some people in the face on a screen. I've been playing a game called *Outer Worlds*, which is made by the same studio that made the *Fallout* games I played after the Giffords shooting, and it's pretty similar, except this one takes place in space. My daughter really wants to play this game, as she can see it's a lot more immersive and realistic than the ones she's mostly allowed to play: though *Cat Quest 2* and *Stardew Valley* are both excellent, they are not quite the same as this kind of high-adrenaline, first-person shooter. You kill some guys. You kill some more guys. You kill some aliens. You blow up space creatures. You whack marauders. You kill really a lot of guys. Some women too. Maybe you can play it where you don't kill guys, but I don't know, and besides, I like killing guys. It satisfies. You do other things too: You make some friends. You help them out. You build a team. You explore all kinds of cool space spaces and unravel plots. You do, if you are me, a lot of quests, almost every one you find. (Something there is in a quest that I cannot resist.)

I send my daughter away when I can tell things are about to get violent. This is often. I don't pursue violence in the game, but you're always in the wake of it. You usually have the option to solve problems by talking and working out solutions, which is what I prefer, both for the feeling of satisfaction and for not wanting to always blast assholes to solve problems, but just as often you end up having to blast people or whatever to make your point, and this becomes more of an issue as you reach the middle of the game and into its final act, where your options winnow down. Then you take their stuff, gathering as much as you can from their corpses, or, if I shoot them with my plasma rifle, a neat little pile of irradiated dust. As I ransacked the quarters of some guy I killed, my daughter asked me: are you stealing?

I'm not *stealing*, exactly. Or, actually, *am* I stealing? I didn't want to have to explain that all this stuff belonged to people I had already killed (I was trying to walk around in a way that prevented her from seeing the bodies I left in my wake: it was hard; there are a lot of them, and it takes a while for them to disappear) or was about to kill. It's only stealing if you take stuff that . . . uh . . . belongs to good guys. To friends. This was not one of my better explanations. The game will punish you if you steal, I explained. Like how? she asked. You can get fined or sent to jail maybe, I responded. They might shoot at me. Friends might become enemies. I didn't say, it rewards you when you kill. The difference between good guy and bad guy, foraging and stealing is, of course, only one of perspective. Like when our erstwhile hero Perseus goes onto Medusa's island in 1981's stop-motion, gods-and-monsters epic *Clash of the Titans* and kills Cerberus, who, while he looked a little scary and had two heads, was only defending his home against invaders like pouty-mouthed hottie Perseus. I mean, Cerberus looked like a pretty good (two-headed) boy, doing what he was supposed to be doing, defending his people, defending his turf. *This is our house*, some sports show somewhere tells us, and it's true: it is, or it was anyhow. I get he's a monster, but that's what happens when you go invading the monster's house: who's the monster now, Perseus? Perseus may be our hero, but what the shit: this is not okay. And anyway, all of this questing and monster-dog killing is prompted by the irritating squabbling of the gods, largely Thetis and Zeus, who seem superannoying, much more so than they seemed to me reading myths in high school.

It's easy to say all of this while watching it, but when you're *playing* the story—when your agency itself makes you the protagonist— it's harder to step back and look at what you're doing when you're doing what you're doing.

What if all game mechanics were changed to never let the bodies disappear? So when you go back to some area where you had to shoot and slash your way through a pile of marauders or space goons or whatever to get more ammo and treasure, you have to wade through the consequences of your actions. Would that be technically difficult to accomplish, keeping track of all those digital corpses? Or has playtesting revealed that—really—nobody wants to have to deal with it?

I think back to another conversation I had with my daughter. She's been playing *Stardew Valley* (largely a farming simulator with a lot of other fascinating mechanics in it), and she explained how she discovered she could buy or make a bomb. The bombs in this game are used for mining or clearing out boulders and rocks and monsters. She was into this idea. Bombs. She said she was going to blow up the village celebration. Wait, what? "You know, the villagers, they all get together for their seasonal celebration and they invite you. It's the best time to bomb them because they're all in the same place. I'm going to blow them all up."

I wasn't sure what to say to that.

It turns out that the game doesn't let you actually bomb the villagers. I've never had the inclination; I tend to play good guys in games. Or, well, I play good characters. Perhaps as a response to masculinity, I never play dudes in games. I always play female characters if I have the choice. Why not rep as something else? I figure. Also I may have had enough of dudes for a while—excepting, obviously, the dudes in *Predator*. My daughter often prefers to play male characters when she has the choice—in games and in her imaginative life—perhaps for a similar set of reasons: to try out, in some small way, some other way of being? I can't blame her: I mean, even now the big epic stories she's exposed to are more likely to have heroes, not heroines.

Writing this book, I can already see how I'm likely going to be pissing off a bunch of easily pissed-off men. We've all watched the fanboys come out to protect their precious pieces of imaginative property against such threats as women and nonwhite actors, and we know how much easier it is to say and do things behind a mask or a screen. While I'd love to watch an all-female remake of *Predator* (kind of like 2005's *The Descent*, actually), I think we can easily imagine how quickly a subset of men would work themselves up into a froth over the idea. Look what happened to that last—and quite good, honestly—*Ghostbusters* with the female cast? I watched all of the harassment of the women involved unfold online, with great embarrassment for my gender. Why do they—we, I guess—*care* so much about this stuff?

I wonder if it's on account of that territorial feeling. That (they believe) they have so few other domains than '80s movie franchises and video games, and that sense of privilege we all grew up on? Of course, all the protagonists in the stories we played or watched or read were dudes. Why wouldn't they be? So when someone comes for one of their most treasured properties, say, *Predator*, and starts pointing to its obvious homoeroticism, they get real mad and start their sputtering. That the movie you love is less straight than you think it is doesn't mean you are less straight than you think you are, guys! It's more complicated than you think it is. You, too, may be more complicated than you think you are, I want to say.

It's also not *your* movie.

Or: this movie may be yours, but it's also ours. It's also mine. *Predator* can be inhabited by whoever wants to claim it for a while, who lets it pull something out of them. Their anger—that feeling of exclusive ownership, and the willingness to bully anyone who wants to claim a little bit of it for themselves—is what makes masculinity tip over into something else. Unfortunately, these guys prove this on every available occasion. That's likely because their territory is continually shrinking. Women in their twenties are asking if there's anything good about masculinity. As the ice floe you're on shrinks, you start to fight whatever you see there to fight. Typically these are not the wisest fights to pick.

So I didn't want to do that. I didn't want to tell these two women at dinner to watch *Predator*, which I couldn't really imagine either of them doing, but maybe I should have. I try to avoid mansplaining when I notice myself clicking into that gear, and this may have been one of those times. "Well," I could have said, "I'm working on a book. Let me tell you about *Predator*..."

SO LET ME TELL YOU MORE about *Predator*. If you didn't know better, watching the movie's establishing shots of Vietnam-era helicopters and the guys in their gear flying in low over an unidentifiable (to my Michigan eyes) jungle, you'd assume this was a Vietnam movie. When *Predator* came out in 1987, America was still in the long hangover from our failures in Vietnam and in the middle of watching many movies about those failures. Look at what was happening in the *Rambo* trilogy (1982, 1985, 1988): the sense of rage and resentment on the part of John Rambo, a Vietnam vet who keeps getting taken advantage of by men in positions of power, is off the charts, and that gets translated into explosions and increasingly silly and highly enjoyable action sequences that get more cartoonish as they go. (*First Blood* remains a serious movie. The others, not so much, but they are worth the watch, if only as cultural artifacts.)

Predator's choppers are the Bell UH-1, the best-known American helicopter in the world, made famous by their use in Vietnam. The Bell UH-1 on display down the road at the Pima Air & Space

Museum has a big red mouth with sharp white teeth painted on it. It looks thrilled and mean, which is, I'm sure, the point. The ones in the movie are unadorned. Since I can't easily get to the Boneyard during the pandemic, I watch a looped video—an "AerialSphere"—of the base on repeat. It's a 360-degree panorama, shot from what looks like a couple of thousand feet, and I can rotate it manually. If I don't, after twenty seconds, it begins rotating slowly. It's fascinating, trying to identify the different types of planes among the thousands on the base, arrayed in different patterns: F-14 Tomcats, F-15 Eagles, A-10 Thunderbolt IIs, C-22As, C-130 Herculeses, C-131 Samaritans, C-141 Starlifters, B-1B Lancers, F-111 Aardvarks, and even civilian planes: 727s, 747s, and so on. I know a lot of these on account of games I used to play and an obsession I had as a kid with World Wars I and II and all of those wars' attendant weaponry. I could identify at one point nearly any twentieth-century American or Soviet warplane. I devoured books about them—for reasons that now feel far away. Why did I care about the Battle of Anzio or the Bulge? Still, it's hard for me not to be awed by these planes all lined up and gleaming in geometric rows. How many trillions of dollars went into these beautiful weapons of war? From above, it's like looking at a collection of models built to scale.

Even from the aerial shot I can see many of these are taped up and in some state of disrepair. The Boneyard classifies these planes according to type: 1000, in long-term storage, to be maintained until recalled to active service; 2000, available for parts reclamation only; 3000, aircraft kept in near flyable condition in short-term, temporary storage; 4000, aircraft "in excess of DoD needs . . . gutted and every usable part has been reclaimed. They will be sold, broken down into scrap, smelted into ingots, and recycled." This is what we do with the tools of war. This also feels a little bit like what my dinner companions were proposing as the future of men.

There are no Bell UH-1s or any helicopters I can see on this part of the base. The only one I see is online in the museum.

On Our Own

SEVEN MINUTES AND FORTY-FIVE SECONDS into the movie, Dillon tells Dutch: there's no backup for the team. They are on their own. Big surprise. There almost never is.

The first of Hawkins's not-good pussy jokes drops shortly thereafter. It is not as funny as he thinks it is, and it takes Billy far too long to get it, creating a weird, awkward silence that means that if we're laughing, we're laughing at his expense. Hawkins, played by Shane Black, is intentionally geeky, a jester sort, bawdy comic relief for the movie. Black, who wrote *Lethal Weapon* and a whole bunch of other movies, and who will go on to direct 2018's flawed-but-better-than-you've-heard sequel *The Predator*, was at the time known primarily as a writer. He was hired here as an actor, but also to have a writer on the set in case some quick rewrites were needed. The jokes are almost certainly all his, and he manages to somehow make the bad joke work.

When Black was asked to do some rewriting work during filming he refused, saying (correctly) he was hired to act, not to write, and perhaps as a result of this refusal to do that work for free, he will be the first of the major characters to get killed off.

In the helicopter we get some verbal sparring among the guys. Much of this movie, like many meetings of men I've been part of, consists of this kind of jockeying for position. It's exhausting as much as it's entertaining. Behind the scenes the actors—all these alpha guys—competed, too, working out in the gym all the time, according to the backstage stories about the film. This is largely a function of Schwarzenegger, who loved and fomented competition. A big part of what makes the movie work as well as it does is the chemistry between the actors. They feel real, like they know each other, like they've worked out some of their self-proving shit already, so we don't have to see *too* much of it on-screen. And they all seem to be enjoying themselves, which comes through in the movie.

If you listen to the DVD commentary by director John McTiernan you'll hear that at first he was displeased with the way the actors were carrying themselves, and he hired a military trainer to come in and run them through actual military training for a few weeks before they started filming, so they would feel more naturally military, and better bonded. McTiernan also tried to cast as many military veterans as he could, which is one reason he got Ventura, a former Navy SEAL. So the cast was pretty well familiar with each other by the time they really started doing scenes.

We're still on the helicopter scene, I know, but on my 144th watching of this movie I *just* get the following joke for the first time. Blain (Jesse Ventura) tells the group that "this stuff" (the tobacco he's chewing) will make you "a god-damned sexual tyrannosaurus just like me." Poncho, gesturing with his large gun, says, "Strap this on your sore ass, Blain." If it's not a good joke, it was a subtle enough wordplay ("tyrannosaurus" / "on your sore ass") to have eluded me for more than thirty years. Finally I've learned to pay attention in school.

Of all the action movie stars of this era, Schwarzenegger is most famous for his one-liners, which became by this point an expectation of the genre. They punctuate the violence, turning what by any standard ought to be a moment of horror or tragedy, as someone gets stabbed or shot or blown up, into comedy. They're asides to the audience, since they're usually directed at us, not at other characters in the scene. They give us permission to laugh before we return to the crazy action. They also helpfully redirect our natural disbelief in the ludicrous nature of what we're seeing into laughing—*with* the movie, not at the movie, which is important. We all get to know it's dumb, this big-gun fun. It's okay, we get to say. We're all on the same side.

Another movie comes to mind: the 2018 film *Mandy*, almost as brilliant as *Predator*. The first half of the movie is an atmospheric, beautifully shot, grueling trip into darkness. Nicolas Cage, deployed here at maximum Nicolas Caginess, is ground down by the brutal killing of his wife, Mandy, and his own near murder at the hands of a cult. So far, so realistic, which makes it pretty tough to take as Mandy is burned alive, upside down, in a sack, with Cage's character bound and forced to watch. It's an intense moment in which we are likewise filled with rage and grief, as he works himself bloodily free and collapses. Right after, this tone gets broken suddenly and totally unexpectedly by a brilliantly weird ad for Cheddar Goblin macaroni and cheese that plays on TV while Cage drinks a lot of vodka and cleans his wounds and screams. It's a goblin-themed Kraft macaroni and cheese knockoff that a weird rubber goblin barfs into the bowls and then over the heads of two hyped-up kids. It's extremely bizarre, superfunny, and is the moment that (for me anyhow) breaks *Mandy* from the familiar and unpleasant genre of exploitation/brutal revenge movie into something else: a totally batshit mystical-action-absurdity-sci-fi revenge movie, and things escalate wildly from there. The joke is the hinge that transforms one half of the movie into the other. Like *Predator*, I could not recommend it any more highly.

Back to our featured presentation.

As we move slowly closer to the team's entry into the jungle, we're also introduced to Mac's weird habit of shaving the sweat off his face with a razor. It's fine if you don't understand what exactly that's meant to tell us. I don't either: is it that he's so manly he doesn't even use shaving cream? That he's so chill he strokes his face with a razor in a helicopter without worry of cutting himself? That he's a weirdo like all these guys probably are? It's as memorable a tic as it is inscrutable, and one that was developed by actor Bill Duke. It does not appear in any version of the script.

As we approach the drop zone, Little Richard is still playing. And I love that the song only goes quiet when Blain shuts off the Sanyo boombox behind his head. *Here's* where the music was coming from, we learn: it's not a soundtrack for us; it's *their* soundtrack. Their boombox. These guys chose their own pump-up song while going off to war. And it's Little fucking Richard! I admire this nice touch of verisimilitude: the song in the film only plays when there's a machine to actually *play* the song in the film. Maybe they liked it so much they listened to it twice: "Long Tall Sally" soundtracks about four minutes of the film, nearly two times the length of the song's 2:07 runtime. Or maybe this tape has it recorded back to back to back, like I used to do with the songs I loved best when I was a kid.

"Long Tall Sally" plays for these boys as they fly into the jungle (and toward most of their deaths, and toward a whole lot of other characters' deaths) *on repeat.*

I really want to explain to the Internet Boy Trolls that Sally, who is Long and Tall and bald-headed and sneaking around in the alley with Uncle John, who is in fact soundtracking these man's men's descent into darkness, is in fact a man.

SO OBVIOUSLY I've become obsessed with *Predator.* And I'm not the only one. Unlike all the other action movies of the '80s, *Predator* has remained the most alive. They made three direct sequels (*Predator 2, Predators, The Predator*) and two crossovers (*Alien vs. Predator* and *Alien vs. Predator: Requiem,* the latter of which is the only one of the franchise I've never managed to make it through: it is that bad). There are a ton of comic book crossovers. Among the most entertaining are *Justice League vs. Predator*; *Superman vs. Predator*; *Motorhead* [evidently not the band, unfortunately] *vs. Predator*; *Aliens vs. Predator vs. The Terminator*; *Predator vs. Magnus, Robot Fighter*; *Tarzan vs. Predator*; *Predator vs. Judge Dredd*; *Batman vs. Predator*; and the original *Aliens vs. Predator*, the latter of which formed the basis for the first *AVP* movie. My favorite is the most stupid-seeming: *Archie vs. Predator*, in which one of the many jokes is that the girls become more vicious than the alien. Ice Cube samples *Predator 2*. There is a whole pile of *Predator* novels, one of which (*Predator: South China Sea*) was written by Jeff VanderMeer, better known for the excellent novel (and underrated movie) *Annihilation*. What is it about *Predator* that keeps us coming back to it? Or what is it about us that keeps these Predators coming back to us? It's almost as if we're not learning the lessons we ought to be.

IT'S DARK AS THEY DISEMBARK. Is it morning? Is it evening? How long have they been listening to Little Richard? This, too, is not important. Our guys are finally on the move. We find the downed chopper. What took it out?

One of the things I love about this movie is how it turns about halfway in, and then it turns again. We think we're watching one thing, and instead we're watching something else, and then something else again. Like with most action movies, action itself becomes a subject. As men, we're almost watching ourselves watching ourselves when we watch action movies: we know their grammar, and know how we respond, and how we're meant to respond, how it gets us pumped up and how we get pumped up about getting pumped up.

While we wait for that something else to be revealed, I also want to note how many of the movie's shots are from odd visual perspectives. Not all of them are artful: they're movie shots. But others bring an aesthetic to the table: here's one following Dillon from above; there's Billy running through the trees, from behind. Here's one in which we pan up trees and consider the sky.

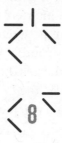

Trying to Forget It

IT'S HARD TO WATCH ASPECTS of the movie while people are in the streets demanding the demilitarization and defunding of the police. It's hard to watch the police's level of armament in 2021 almost match *Predator*'s level. It's hard to watch America burn and turn on itself, and to watch armed men storm the US Capitol. I'm having a hard time revisiting this movie—which is a site of pleasure and mystery for me—against a backdrop of what the fuck, and knowing well that some of these guys (mostly guys) doing these terrible things have surely watched and rewatched *Predator*. What did they *see* when they watched *Predator*? Do they see the same things I do when I watch it now? I mean, *Predator* is a tool through which America sees itself, or has the *opportunity* to see itself if it's paying attention.

In the twenty years leading up to 1987, the United States explicitly or covertly invaded or entangled itself in Grenada, Angola, Poland, Nicaragua, Haiti, Afghanistan, Cambodia, Lebanon, Libya, El Salvador, Kuwait, Laos, Chile, and this list goes on for a long time. Viewers of *Predator* on its release would have been aware of some, if not all of these entanglements, at least in theory. According to political scientist Dov Levin of Carnegie Mellon University, the United States attempted to interfere at least eighty-one times in foreign presidential elections between 1946 and 2000. "That number doesn't include military coups and regime change efforts following the elections of candidates the U.S. didn't like, notably . . . in Iran, Guatemala and Chile," the *LA Times* tells us, citing Levin's work in an article. Later, Blain will tell Mac that this jungle "makes Cambodia look like Kansas."

Many of these entanglements were invisible to most Americans, perhaps because we weren't really paying attention. As a kid, obviously I paid these things little attention, taking the Reagan years and the Cold War at face value, basically the plot of *Rocky IV*, and I'd only understand later how dark our foreign policy actually was—and had been for a very long time. But *Predator* knows it.

At 14:50 we get one of the movie's two explicit acknowledgments of the United States' history of fucked-up foreign entanglements. Poncho says to Dutch, "Guerrillas and two men in the chopper, followed by men with American equipment. Do you remember Afghanistan?" We see actual pain and uncertainty in the silence following this line. After all, these guys are here in a foreign country on uncertain terms. They're on their own, as we've learned. They know what the American military is capable of, and to what dark ends it has been used before. So what are they actually doing here anyway, and why? The question echoes.

But Dutch doesn't seem interested in engaging, so we'll leave that thought suspended for a little bit. He responds with a smile. "Trying to forget it. C'mon." The tension passes.

I'm not going to point out *all* the homoerotic imagery in this movie, but once you start watching through that lens, you can't stop seeing it. Just a few seconds later, we see Billy hacking a stiff vine in half. He holds the cut end to his mouth, sucking on it to get it started. Then he senses something else in the jungle and turns a bit. The vine drips a viscous white fluid on the side of his face.

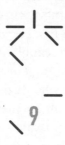

So Many Easier Ways to Hurt

SIXTEEN MINUTES IN and we're confronted with the first unearthly horror of the film: a jump scare. It's three of the guys the
team is meant to rescue, hung upside down from trees and *skinned*.
It's a gruesome sight and a compelling effect. And it's also in-
explicable: as Paul Monette writes in the novelization: "Why strip a
man of his skin? Why bother? There were so many easier ways to
hurt." The line from the novelization is echoed shortly after in the
film. Poncho asks, "They skinned them? Why did they *skin* them?"

Have I told you yet about Paul Monette? He wrote the novelization of *Predator*, released alongside the movie in 1987. The novelization is a critically unloved art form, meant to be consumed
by people who want to read a movie, whatever that means, instead
of or after seeing it. They're produced on the fly, often from an
early version of the screenplay. They are not released in hardcover
with deckle edges and French flaps and blurbs from fancy writers. Novelizations are not meant to be artful or prestigious: they're
meant to be fast. If you had to wait until the script was absolutely
finished before giving it to the writer, it wouldn't be possible to get
the book out in time to coordinate with the movie.

Paul Monette was best known as a poet, and eventually as a memoirist who would go on to win a National Book Award in nonfiction for *Becoming a Man*. He was also a gay man. I discovered Monette in a 1999 grad school poetry workshop in which we read books of elegies, including *Love Alone: Eighteen Elegies for Rog*, Rog being his partner who died of complications related to AIDS. The one big data point I remember from someone doing a presentation on Monette for that class was "and he also wrote the novelization for *Predator*." Wait, what?

I didn't make much of it at the time except as an odd fact, but it stuck in me somewhere. Writers gotta work, and work he did. This wasn't Monette's first novelization or his first Hollywood experience: he worked on screenplays for many years with his writing partner. He was probably best known as a screenwriter, in fact, until *Love Alone*. I loved and admired the poems in *Love Alone*, though what a twenty-six-year-old straight man got out that book was surely only a slice of what was happening there. What I remember from it was Monette's enveloping grief and incendiary rage at his powerlessness and the world's inability to do anything to ease Rog's or his own suffering, all spliced into moments of great sadness and beauty. It's a hard and good book to read. It holds up well.

What I would find out only later was that that Monette wrote the *Predator* novelization *as* Rog was dying of AIDS, and *as* he was writing *Love Alone*. In fact he tells us that he was working on *Predator* while he sat beside his dying partner's bed in a California hospital, trying to find something, even something big and dumb and stupid, to keep him occupied.

Love Alone still hits me hard, perhaps in part because it connects more deeply to me at forty-five than it did at twenty-six, being that I'm married with a kid and can imagine much deeper forms of loss than I could then. But I also now know a great deal more about Monette and the AIDS crisis and the US government's refusal to look at it or talk about it or even name it for far, far too long. AIDS—and its effect on gay men in particular—was ignored by the US government, or at least those in power refused to look at it directly (and by so doing are complicit in the body count).

I didn't read Monette's novelization then (why would I read *any* novelization? I was in grad school, a Serious Art Person, or liked to front like I was around other Serious Art People, who may also in retrospect have been similarly fronting). I was not a great student. At that point I hadn't discovered the pleasure of following weird questions about marginal phenomena as far as I could take them. I didn't know nonfiction was even something anyone who wasn't in their sixties wrote, much less about subjects as trivial and dumb as action films.

A decade later, I wondered: What was this award-winning, nationally renowned, now dead gay poet *doing* writing *Predator*?

IN THE FILM, when Blain calls the other guys "slack-jawed faggots" in the chopper scene, it wounds me a little now. You can see it on my face as the movie plays. I don't know how it felt to hear it then, but it wasn't unusual in the '80s (not to the decade's credit) and even in my social circle then, which, admittedly, consisted largely of teenage boys. We did not pay attention to the way the things we said wounded our friends—or wounded us. This is one of the only moments in the movie that reminds me what the 1980s were, and that reminds me of how much this was an artifact of its time. I mean, it doesn't stop my watching, but it doubles it up: I'm watching 1987 and I'm watching me in 1987. I mean, I watch it all the time. But every time that one line comes up it pushes the needle a little deeper. It was in the script—it wasn't improvised. In fact, it was in a version of the script two years earlier, back when most of the characters had slightly different names. In the 1985 script, Dillon is Dixon. Hawkins is Murphy. Mac is Williams (though in this version of the script, he's meant to be even bigger than Blain). Poncho is Ramirez. Dutch is Matheny. Billy is Miguel. Blain remains Blain. But slack-jawed faggots remain slack-jawed faggots.

I think this moment is an attempt to caricature Blain, the biggest of the big boys, as *particularly* macho, really trying to prove something, even amidst these obviously apex macho dudes, all of whom will have their shirts off at some point during the next one hundred minutes. The more dudes are in the movie and the more shirtless they all are, the more the movie needs to suggest that this isn't as homoerotic as it obviously is.

In the script, the moment is described like this: "It's an old gag but they obviously care for [Blain] in a big way." The novelization doesn't reproduce this remark. The whole interchange is mostly affectionate, I guess, like a lot of what some presidents refer to as locker-room talk. Lots of bad shit gets cloaked in affection, a lesson I keep having to learn myself. I definitely called friends faggots—affectionately, I want to tell myself: they *were* my friends. Wait, *were* they my friends? Was I *their* friend?

A few years after I first watched *Predator* my family moved to Riyadh, Saudi Arabia, for my dad's job. He was working for the American government as an economic adviser to the Saudi government for something called JECOR: the US–Saudi Arabian Joint Commission on Economic Cooperation. I never thought it odd at the time, but in retrospect it sounds a little bit—and my wife and I have definitely entertained the thought—like a cover for some kind of CIA situation. Was my dad in the CIA, or "in CIA," as the CIA puts it? I've never asked him (not that he'd tell me if he was, at least if he was any good at what he was doing), and I don't think so, but the fact is that we spent several years in Riyadh, a city and country about as far away from forested, snowbound, rural, white Upper Michigan as I can imagine another place being.

We lived on an American and international compound, and my brother and I were friends with a bunch of the kids there, and we fucked around doing whatever.

Probably for self-preservation, my memory obscures a lot of who I was then, but I clearly remember two things, both of which make me feel like an asshole now. I was friends with this kid named Alejandro, but for some reason I decided (maybe it was we, but I think it was I) to call him Bucky, which he didn't like. I was able to convince a bunch of our friends and even his dad to start calling him Bucky, which I thought was very entertaining (but was surely just bullshit bullying). And I made up a dumb (even then I knew it was dumb) rap about another friend, Amr: "Yo my name is Amr, I'm a major fag; if you don't believe me, just look at my tag. See: Amr? See: fag. Huh huh huh huh huh. Told ya." It's superbad on so many levels, and I find it very embarrassing to write it here now, one reason I've never told anyone or written about it. I don't know why I even retain this particular piece of my own assholery. I'm sure there were plenty of others. Kids—well, maybe boys? White boys? White boys growing up in Michigan? Or assholes like me? I'm unsure how far to extrapolate from my own experience—kids do accumulate these instances of assholery. I was the object of many of them myself, not being, let's be honest, the most masculine boy in any room pretty much ever. If we're lucky, we forget these instances as we discard parts—or whole shells—of who we used to be. It may be that I remember these two things because some part of me *wants* to remember them, to remind myself of what an asshole I was. I mean, sure, I was thirteen; it's not a great age for nuance and empathy. But that was also a year I watched and rewatched *Predator*, so it hit me where I was then, back when, oh baby, I was having some fun tonight, whatever that meant to me then. I was having some fun. I was shooting some guns. The more I replay that fun, though, the less fun it seems.

Maybe I'm making too much of a dumb joke in a movie. The Internet Boy Trolls sure tell me so. But I don't wish it wasn't in the movie: *Predator* might be a more comfortable movie for me without it, but our cultural artifacts are ours, and my assholery is mine, and we ought to own what we watched and listened to and said and made, and part of what I'm watching when I'm watching the movie is us (is me), and it does feel good (it's odd to say) to be reminded that this is where we were, even if to some degree, this is also where a lot of us still are.

Other than that joke, *Predator* mostly wears its age well enough. Sure, it relies on ethnicity and race to characterize. But, like many '80s movies, it also has good roles for actors of color, and it doesn't draw undue attention to its diverse cast. Richard Chaves, playing Poncho, is actually of Cherokee descent, IMDb tells me. Sonny Landham, playing Billy, a character whose "spiritual connection" to the world rests a little too easily on received ideas about Native Americans, was in fact part Cherokee and Seminole, not that the writers probably knew the difference. There are multiple Black characters: Mac, played by the glorious Bill Duke, gets maybe the best role in the movie, and Carl Weathers gets plenty to do as redeemed antagonist Dillon. You can't say a lot about the roles for women in the film (with only one role this is never going to pass the Bechdel test), but Anna, played by Elpidia Carrillo, is one of only two characters who will survive, and she's no simple victim either. That these characters all seem to have some depth, that they feel lived-in and relational is one of the things that makes the movie work as well as it does. These characters don't feel like caricatures. This is very unusual in action films (it's unusual in most films, actually), and it portrays intimacy between the men in particular in ways that feel to me real, even thirty-three years later.

Rereading Monette's *Predator* novelization at thirty-eight was an odd experience. Sure, he did it for the money, but he also did it for the glory, at least in part, since it was Hollywood. His partner was fucking *dying* in front of him while the world—or the public American world, anyhow—refused to even acknowledge that HIV and AIDS were real, much less existential threats. Maybe it felt good to concentrate on something seemingly mindless like *Predator*.

But how could he have avoided the obvious comparison? Like the protagonists in the film, Monette, his partner, and nearly everyone in his life were also being pursued by an invisible and unstoppable predator, one officially unacknowledged by authorities. They, too, were on their own, no backup, in their fight. The fight would be to the death for most of them, and like *Predator* it was all about the men.

The novelization form dates back at least to the late nineteenth century, though it became much more popular in the 1910s with the rise of cinema as a popular art form and the advent of the movie serial (an evolution of narrative prose serials in periodicals) as opposed to the longer "feature." As literature was a popular commercial art form at the time and film was still relatively inaccessible, many films in this time were accompanied by prose recaps published in newspapers and magazines designed to entice the public to return for the next chapter of the film serial, according to an article by Ben Singer in *Film History*. Sometimes these serial recaps would be collected into books and sold, and eventually, these narrative recaps would skip serialization and published as books, as with 1915's *Les Vampires*, one of the first book-length novelizations of a popular film. As film supplanted prose as the most popular form of entertainment, this relationship shifted, with serials moving from prose to screen and novelizations now serving as ways of capturing those films in print, since films moved quickly from theater to theater until their reels wore out. A century later, there is still a significant commercial market for novelizations of popular films.

Even knowing that there are often significant differences between films and their novelizations due to novelizers' having to work from preproduction scripts, I was struck by how different the *Predator* book is from the movie in crucial and at times unsettling ways: for instance, in the novelization, the Predator can actually assume the *physical form* of other creatures, or at least any creature *without a soul*, Monette tells us. And because it *can't* assume a human form (presumably on account of our having souls), it's fascinated with us and our behavior, and tries to understand, and *that* (at least partly) is why it kills and collects us, in search of understanding, you know, like how trophy hunters explain how their work is really conservation or science or whatever.

I was also surprised by how beautiful Monette's novelization is, on its own, but also how it illuminates the source material, that source material being the screenplay and script, not the movie, which he had not, of course, seen when he wrote it. Reading it I understood what a poet saw in *Predator*, watching and reimagining it from the inside. Here are some of the passages I love best, presented as a list that I had to end early, or else it would be half the book:

> Unstated of course, perhaps not even conscious, but these guys were always proving something. You didn't drink a pint of whiskey if somebody else was packing away a fifth.

> They were only alive in action, and they needed one another the way they needed guns.

> Now and then out here a thing got so gigantic it grew unearthly— an orchid, a grasshopper, sometimes a frog.

> It [the Predator] was like a lost soul searching for a form in which to flower.

> And twined through it all like the grip of a vine in a cotton-wood tree was the certainty of death—their mates', their enemy's, their own. A match had been lit deep in the mine, and the fuel that would feed the fire might turn out to be the whole dark earth itself.

> It surveyed Blain and Mac with its heat-seeking vision, their bodies outlined in luminous aureoles.

I could go on with this all day. I've transcribed more than twenty pages of my favorite passages. I mean, there's lots of bad

writing in there too. He relies way too much on race and ethnicity to orient us to character. We're told over and over that Mac and
Duke are Black, that Poncho is Chicano and "from the Barrio,"
and when we get to Billy, well, we'll talk about that later. I chalk
a lot of this up to 1987, having to work from an unfinished script,
and not getting to see what the film actually does to bring these
stereotypes to life.

In spite of that, if you read the novelization you'll see there's
plenty of glory for Monette. He didn't need to make it beautiful;
he only needed to make it fast. Yet he did both things. Did he find
the story itself beautiful? Or did he find a way to locate beauty
in the story? Maybe as a poet he couldn't stop himself from ori-
enting toward beauty in whatever guises he could find it.

Monette wasn't only a poet, of course, but a gay man, attuned
to watching men in ways I was not attuned to watching men (there
is plenty more of that breathless male-on-male gaze like you see in
the last quote). And, what's more, reading *Predator*, I saw what
a poet—one whose partner was dying from an invisible and unstoppable disease at the very same time he was trying to work on
this dumb book—saw or was able to find in a dumb action movie.

"Say it clearly and you make it beautiful, no matter what,"
Bruce Weigl, another poet, writes. I think that's right. I believe it:
look closely enough at a thing and it is beautiful, because it's you
seeing it that makes it beautiful. Or maybe you're made beautiful
by seeing it clearly. It's what that thing—however dumb or point-
less it may seem to others—reveals in you that matters.

A few years back, I interviewed Jacob Slichter, memoirist and
the drummer from the '90s band Semisonic (best known for their
massive hit, "Closing Time," which is in my view still a brilliant
song, even if it's not the best song on that album; I'll take "Singing
in My Sleep" every day). As part of that conversation I was playing
him some '90s songs I was thinking about at the time, and how
they resonated with me, and he got very pumped up when I played
him Joan Osborne's song "One of Us":

In spite of its clunkiness, it's too awesome to deny. It's like Chicago. "Question[s] 67 [and] 68" by Chicago. You're embarrassed by the lyrics, and yet it pulls something out of you that—you know—is just too . . . it's more important that that thing gets pulled out of me than the fact that I'm embarrassed that it happens.

Now, I know the band Chicago only in passing, and from their not-great '80s ballads, largely, so I did cue up the song after, hearing his obvious excitement for it. What was this song that so turned him on? I have to say it left me cold. There were a lot of horns and I'm pretty sure Peter Cetera, whom I can't take seriously after his '80s cheese, even if he did wear a Bauhaus shirt in the video for max-cheese "You're the Inspiration." This Chicago song did have some prog-rock shifts that I guess are kind of fun, but it felt like music for a movie I had no interest in ever seeing. It's a generational thing, I'm sure. Slichter is a few years older than me, and we all know how the things we loved at fourteen imprint themselves upon us.

The things we loved at fourteen were made by and of the world we inhabited at fourteen. If that world has embedded itself in us, then it's embedded itself in a whole generation of usses. Let a couple of decades go by and you get a world shaped by and around—for better or worse—the things embedded in us and in the rest of us in thousands of ways, only some of which are visible, even if you look.

I believe that if you look hard and long enough at what you loved best at fourteen and how you lived then and what you saw in the world, it will reveal both the world and you. Or maybe you'll exhaust it, or it'll exhaust you.

This is my fear, my friends: that after all of this, eventually *Predator* will leave you cold.

Actually, that's not it: my fear is that *Predator* will eventually leave *me* cold.

Or maybe what I really fear is that, like my mother, *Predator* will leave me in the cold.

But the alternative to the Slichter equation is unpalatable: it's more important that the thing gets pulled out of me than the fact that I'm embarrassed it happens. I can't simply leave it there unexamined and hope it goes away. It's embarrassing to admit that I've seen the movie 146 times, to write so much about *Predator*, to show how much it means to me, to explain how much I learned about masculinity by watching it, to demonstrate how deeply it has wounded me, and to share with you how much it gives me joy every time I think of it. I mean, I wouldn't be doing this if I didn't have to.

Writing this it's hard not to flash back to the famous face-hugger scene from *Alien*, and more specifically the panic after: what is the thing that attached itself so powerfully to us, and why did it drop off right after? What did it leave of itself inside us? And where did it go? What will it do to us the longer whatever's inside us remains interior?

On Infrared

You found the [thermal imaging camera], now you must start the [Predator book].   —RICHARD HUGO

THE MOST LASTING and recognizable of *Predator*'s many great effects is this one: the thermal imaging we see ourselves through. This is the first point of the movie's transformation into something else. The camera tracks us (our protagonists) into the trees, and then we switch into an infrared shot that tracks two of our team and then the whole group as they move through the jungle. These shots are beautiful and surprising. We see our bodies in a way we hadn't previously imagined. I don't remember if I'd ever seen humans through infrared before, though I probably had, since I understood immediately that it was our heat that we were seeing.

So many of my favorite shots from this film come in infrared. They nearly all take work to comprehend: an art effect. I'm not used to seeing palms and brush outlined in washes of winter blue, and the flatness of our bodies rainbow-bright in stripes and patches of pink and red and orange. It's disorienting, and each shot has to teach us how to read it, and has to give us time to resolve what we're seeing. Seeing—and recognizing—becomes what we *do* in most of these shots, especially the early ones, where we're still learning, and we don't yet know whose eyes we're seeing through.

This is probably the time to mention that the more I watched *Predator* and thought about it seriously over the past decade, the more reasonable it began to seem to me to buy an infrared camera myself so that I could replicate the movie's landmark visual spectacle and apply it to my life. So I did. The sliver of radiation that humans' eyes can parse is small, which *Predator* illustrates with its outstanding cam effect: through it we see how the thing sees what we cannot. To get the creature's POV is rare in action films, or any kind of film in fact: through it we see ourselves. How often do we get to see—to really *see*—how the other sees? How we look to someone else? To it?

It's a gift, I'm telling you, and when we see ourselves through the creature's eyes, that's where we begin to sympathize with the thing that stalks us. Be in another's POV and it changes you a little. Science has proved what readers know: that when we read we *experience*, gain a couple of points of empathy. We live as another thing, in another time. So when we see as it, we become it, if in some small part. We need the tools to see ourselves from outside ourselves now more than ever, because we're increasingly bad at it. If the tool's an action film, I'll take the action film and direct it at my head.

Really, it's remarkable that we can see at all. Animals of every other sort are far more sensitive to the wavelengths of the world than we are. Even my daughter knows how little we can see: she tells me cats can see some ultraviolet that we can't, and don't even get her started on birds. We're so central to our stories that our paucity remains very difficult to believe. We only figured out a decade ago that elephants communicate using superlow frequencies, well below what we can hear: with their ears, for thousands of years, they have been sending messages from miles and miles away. Until then we figured that they didn't have so much to say. Since they didn't speak to us, we figured they weren't speaking at all.

These limited spectra of ROYGBIV—poor and remote as they are—are ours: our climes, our hills, our stamp sand and our sunken dredge, our abandoned mines and the towns around them, our shot-down congresswomen, our broken, potholed roads on which we drive in our crappy 1987 Aerostars until, rusted through, they drive no more and, lo, we mourn their passing. At least on the roads we know, we presume we hold home-field advantage.

Nope: Enter the creature with thermal vision, camouflage. Advantage: Predator until it dawns on Dutch, accidentally covered in cooling mud and so invisible to it (never mind that trick would work for, like, a minute only), that the creature sees his body heat not him. (Is that an analog for an actor's life? Is that an analog for mine?)

The alien, as in most films, gets used to its advantage and underestimates its foe, our hero, and will be eventually killed for our delight. Some humans are exceptional, we understand. We aren't all chaff, bags of lie down and die, cheese-covered fries sprawled like bodies across a plate you ate from last week and Instagrammed and still regret. You should. It was a lot and like your photostream you're still filled with its culinary glory.

Since then what I've wanted most to know is this: what would it take, be like, to see in infrared that way?

Well, reader, I bought the camera. It cost $270. It arrives tomorrow. I anticipate my new eyes and my transformation. In the interim, on the disc golf course with my daughter in a running stroller, a dude walks up to me. At first I read the man approaching as a threat and I go into defensive mode. I'm disc golfing: I have no time to bleed. But then it's revealed he's up to something else. Unsolicited, he hands me a hundred dollar bill. Says, "Sometimes you just need a little help." This is true. I look around for the candid camera crew, but don't see one. Huh. So I say thanks, and take it as an endorsement of my project and my poetics.

I don't know about you, but with my thermal camera my eyes have changed and so my I has changed. I'm sure of it. I see new. I'm seen. I'm something new. I'm trying anyway. By now I've convinced myself you've never seen anything like me before. You haven't, have you? Lie to me if necessary.

THERE ARE SO MANY SHOTS like this in the movie where what we're seeing is the creature's thermal vision adjusting. What is it we're supposed to be seeing? We can't yet tell. What is it we're doing? We're *understanding*. We're recognizing. I watch this happen in slow motion on repeat. I love the moment between the seeming thing and the thing that it becomes, so I keep rewatching this bit on a loop, repeating the procedure: isn't it fascinating coming to terms with the very act of perception? I love those Magic Eye 3D images for this reason, how you know there's something else there, and if you can only work your eyes just right you start to see an edge of that other image, and then it pops you recognize its shape and you can't see anything else. Or, go back further to an older technology, the stereoscope, two slightly different shots of the same image that when you get your eyes to focus on them, they create an actual 3D effect from a 2D image. I've been spending a lot of hours training myself by looking at these.

Good watching works like this: I perceive one thing but when I look more closely, tracing one edge or one feature, I see something else within that thing. It's humbling that I'm doing when I do this: I remind myself that what I think I see may not be all there is. It's why, when I reread a book at forty-five I read a different book from the one I read at thirty-five or twenty-five. The book hasn't changed, but the reader has. This fact gives me hope, and even if the most obvious takeaway from these shots remains the same (the creature sees the team but they can't see the creature), these shots are really about adaptation, our ability to see ourselves as others do, and to—hopefully—evolve, at least a little.

I even love the interference, the noise—is it digital or is it analog? I can't tell—in the effect. In fact, it's abstraction I'm watching when I'm watching this, and it's easy for me to lose my footing the longer I stay.

Jam a pattern on another and trace the interference, feed the resulting data to the system; I can't yet make out a face in this shot but something in it's opening up to me. Even though I know it may be how sprites deteriorate as the processor slows under extreme load I start to think there's signal in its noise. We see what we prefer to see: our memories' edits of the last time we accessed these events. Edit: *accessed* obscures it with a metaphor—blame the computer age, the source of many convenient ways we've tried to deputize the world. To live we must believe that there are somewhere, somehow, static data deep in storage that we call facts slash history slash the past comma verifiable. So what if, when magnified, remembering disintegrates?

We were so concerned with memory in 1987 that to access it we tried hypnosis, guided retrieval of memories that proved we had to be products of ritual abuse at our parents' hands—they turned out to be Satanists, didn't they? (Remember: as we imagine, we remember; and as we remember, we imagine.) That was some dark shit then, wasn't it?

Don't ask Monette. He had other tragedies to occupy his time. But from three decades on, in the league of disturbing phenomena I'd rank the Satanic Panic pretty high. Still can't grok it fully. Tweet @angermonsoon if you have a satisfying theory #regardinghuman weaknessorhysteria #thefallibilityofmemory. I'm still worried: I don't want to be near me if I'm capable of that sort of self-delusion. Except obviously I am. You are too, Boo. That's what watching *Predator means*: even when it looks at itself it cannot see itself. (How much of ourselves can we ever see?) When Dutch looks at the alien, does he see the many guys he killed with his technological and physical superiority? Does he see what all those other nameless extras saw in him? What makes Schwarzenegger different from the thing, except that his blankness is a little bit more like ours?

It's Monette's glass on the nightstand in the Paul Monette museum where we can gape at who we used to want to be and so what if we fell prey to mission creep along the way, fucked by time and story? Was it fear or our desire that led us here, thirty years and innumerable beers post-*Predator*, to the shrine of ritual abuse and recovered memory, unable to disambiguate real toads from imaginary gardens, the Magic from the Johnson or the marker, Marianne from Julianne from Michael Moore? I'm still waiting by the screen for the ghost to show since I first ran this algorithm ten years ago (I tried to kill the process in the intervening decade a hundred times and it would not subside) but nothing yet. It's stars and dark and static. I bet it comes out only when I sleep. I don't have faith in much: it's automatic how hard and deep I doubt. What's inside the film of form is not only randomness. Chide me if you must. I have ideas. Sometimes they drive the line; sometimes they don't. I won't apologize for this or anything. I mean, I should apologize for everything but can't. If I didn't want, I'd die.

I'm broken, too, like *Breakin' 2: Electric Boogaloo Live on Ice* streaming only partly dubbed from some Russian server.

OFF-SCREEN, THIRTEEN MILES AWAY from the Tucson Safeway where my congresswoman was shot, is the International Wildlife Museum (IWM), a trophy hall turned kind-of-educational institution built to resemble a castle, complete with battlements. Approaching it, my impression is that it's ready to be defended, I guess, against invasion, though who might want to invade I couldn't tell you.

Inside I find more than a thousand dead animals largely shot, trapped, or otherwise killed by men, though signs say that in its recent years the museum has primarily received animals that have died natural deaths. It's hard to know how much of this to believe, since, like most museums, this one has a story to tell: every apex predator—lion, tiger, bear—is posed in its most threatening position, though they were more likely shot while fleeing, sleeping, or drinking from a water hole.

Signs also tell me that the IWM is "a nonprofit educational institution dedicated to increasing knowledge and appreciation of the world's wildlife" and "a program of the Safari Club International Foundation . . . that funds and manages worldwide programs dedicated to wildlife conservation, outdoor education and humanitarian services." Sure, but it's also something else: a site of horror and wonder, the bodies of hundreds of animals, drained of blood and stuffed and mounted. Its other story is obsession.

By animals I mean basically only their skins, wrapped around some kind of Styrofoam. Even their lively eyes are glass. I mean, all these are outlines we're seeing: the shapes of animals. I mean that if you want to see your wildlife alive, you are definitely in the wrong place.

Halfway through, I find McElroy Hall, named after C. J. McElroy, "a big game trophy collector with a sixth-grade education who claimed to be the greatest hunter in the world." The Predator says that may or may not be true, but McElroy did found the IWM and the Safari Club International and reportedly collected more than 415 trophies over a fifty-plus-year hunting campaign on six continents. In his hall you'll find nearly 250, 200 of which are the cutoff heads of grazing animals. The southern wall alone holds 112, including the heads of the smallest sorts of deer: the royal antelope, the oribi, the Salt's dik-dik, the Livingstone's suni. Such tiny things: they look like baby animals to me.

It's a hell of a spectacle: it's a spectacle and it's a hell. The man (and by extension all men, I guess) had a mania for death, and paying admission to this place makes me party to it. It's awful and it's not. The experience of seeing so many wild things unwilded and up close unlocks in me a childlike mode: I do want to touch the bear's fur and put my foot up on the crocodile, and here you can, and so I do. But when I touch a dead animal, what am I touching? All the things that make it animal have been stripped away.

The room's intended to overwhelm, and three leather couches are provided. (I am particularly conscious that these also were once animal.) Do I sit or not? What does sitting make me more complicit in?

Up to this point in the museum we've only seen groups of animals posed together. Each tells a story: a hyena steals an egg. A leopard carries off a young killed deer. Three wolves leap on a fallen reindeer who looks at you with a what-the-fuck expression. Down the hall a bobcat swipes a quail and will always swipe a quail. It will swipe and swipe and swipe until it falls apart.

In McElroy Hall, this time it's personal. Sit here and feel the man's mania for blood. The evidence is everywhere; it adds up fast. Anywhere you sit or stand in the room an animal seems to look at you. The East African greater kudu makes eyes at me in a disapproving way. The sing sing waterbuck appears to offer some pity. The scimitar-horned oryx, the southern roan antelope, and the Limpopo bushbuck look and tell me nothing new. The Nile bushbuck and the bontebok stare at me but seem to see right through me. Of course they do not see. Here there's only seems.

I give in and sit. I don't know why I pull out my thermal imaging camera again but I do. I scan the room and all the heads. Through this filter there seems to be nothing here. Nothing shows except the soft glow of rows of ceiling lights. I wave my hand in front of it, and am startled to see my own hand's heat. What did I expect to see? Why am I so disturbed by this? Even the Predator would take no interest in things that have no heat.

Seeing my own heat reminds me that I am alive and these animals are not. They seemed fearsome and now they're dead. Even if I didn't have anything to do with their killing, I can touch their room-temperature corpses, and I do, and I can't help but feel filled by the human power we assume: if you want apex predators, we're it: we kill the apex predators. We put them in a museum.

Little wonder that we're fascinated by those who kill us: the Predator, for sure, but earthly killers too. You can visit the Villisca

Axe Murder House in Iowa, the Wyoming Frontier Prison, the Bonnie and Clyde Ambush Museum, the Alcatraz East Crime Museum, Italy's Serial Killer Museum, the Lombroso Museum of Criminal Anthropology in Turin, and the Museums of Death in New Orleans and Los Angeles. You can take a 3.5-hour tour of the Manson murders. Visit the bar where Aileen Wuornos had her last drink as well as the motel in which she killed one of her victims. You can take the Cream City Cannibal Tour and walk through Milwaukee's streets where Jeffrey Dahmer lured seven of his victims. Stay at the Lizzie Borden bed and breakfast in Massachusetts. Take two different true-crime tours in Seattle: the Capitol Hill Tour and the Queen Anne Tour to get the history between Ted Bundy and Robert Yates. There's a Zodiac Killer Tour in San Francisco. I've been on gruesome ghost tours in New Orleans and in London and in Bisbee, Arizona.

Cut back to the McElroy room and the small case I find in its corner that contains twenty-seven skulls, in increasing size from skunk to bobcats, mongoose to badger, culminating in a bunch of bears. I turn my camera on it and of course it shows me nothing but a ghost of my own reflection.

I imagine the alien walking through this place, trying to understand what the children are even looking at. What the fuck is there to see here anyway? The story it tells about the culture that made it is not a positive one except to show how strange we humans are: we kill these things in droves. We let them cool. We skin them, clean them, throw away most of what made the animal the animal, and fasten the skin on tubes of plastic, steel, and Styrofoam so that they somewhat resemble, at least in their pose, the familiar things that we dream haunt us. Then they haunt us anyway, and what haunts us cannot be shot. If it doesn't bleed, we can't kill it.

I mean, this is a story of obsession and predation: McElroy's, and also ours. After all, I am here. And, reading this, you are too. We both pay in different ways.

All of these beasts were once alive, and now they're furniture, much like the leather couch. Even McElroy is dead: at first I'm surprised he didn't have his own corpse stuffed and perched at the center of the room so he could forever gaze proudly at all the things he killed.

Another story, though: McElroy is also no more alive than the 415 animals he killed.

I imagine him before his death, sitting here in this very spot after the museum had closed, quietly looking and reliving, the privilege of the predator. Through their blank eyes, did he see his death? Did he see himself differently? Did he see himself at all? Why collect eyes if they don't help you see something you could not before?

McElroy would have made a fine trophy for the Predator; I for one would root for the Predator.

When I sit here as he did, am I him? Is that what the room is meant to do, make me play his role? I think so. But I don't *feel* like a predator in here. I don't feel obsessed, and even if I can't see it with my thermal camera, I feel the heat of his obsession. I have my moment, for what it's worth to the dead things here. Then it's broken, as a few grown men walk in, and I feel like a child again among them. I turn my infrared camera on the men to be sure they are what they seem. They have heat: they aren't just meat. I listen. Coming in they were explaining things to each other back and forth, but then they got quiet. Like me they stared up at the walls and had nothing to say, at least for a moment. They seemed as powerless as me, and equally as subject to the story of the room. Here we're all small; we are all children stumbling in a world of men. This is the fruit of the fantasia of the gun.

Strange, Major

AT 17:30, Dutch asks, "What happened here, Billy?"

Billy prefaces his reply by saying, "Strange, Major." The major is strange, and the situation is strange. If the creature cannot shift form, the movie can, and we'll go through a couple of metamorphoses on our way to the skeletal final form we arrive at in the end.

I pause the film on this shot, Billy looking out at the jungle, seeing—or sensing—something, everything strangely still. As I look at it, I'm reminded of a line from a Mary Szybist poem that for some reason I misread at first as beginning with *Doritos*:

> [Doritos are] God's entrance into time:
> time meaning history, meaning a body.

In my experience, most poems can be improved when you misread them with Doritos, as action movies and television can. If I stare long enough at the screen and let my eyes adjust, I start to see things differently:

The vengeful one the silent one the one that watches us invisibly from trees, listening, sifting language clipped from cell phone convos captured on account of a couple of errant words—a threat to the president offered as a joke—and flagged and databased and now attention's paid to what and whom I sext and SMS and how that compares to the accumulating data on my actions versus everyone's actions and how the algorithm wants to interpret it— and even if it disappears in this age, what does disappearing mean?

The one considering our blood's speed, how heavily armed we are, and what we've done and need and what we're capable of not only now in time but *anytime*—saying it, not knowing what it means but shivering the flavor of the sound of *time* in its mouth— diphthong and emblem of M, nacho cheesier for the algorithm eater.

Or maybe not God the brand the cred-encrusted indie band but *a* god, grass-fed and many-legged, begging, one of the hundred thousand household gods who underwrite our volts and insulate our hearts from electric strike since, dumb, we swim in storm-strewn pools in full sight of lightning less than a half hour after eating.

The gods who guarantee our safeties are on before we click them off and finger triggers to fire at whatever moves because we're moved to fire and filled with it, desire for fire (this is how we show we matter, by burning or being burned, by gunplay with our homies, cherry bombing bathrooms with our homies), or movement through the scrub surrounding the Safeway hubbub where no one pretends not to know we're packing and so lonely.

Maybe I mean the minor ones, those junior Predators not yet of age and out to prove something to themselves on this wack planet: what do they want from us aside from trophies and extreme artificial flavors and to emulate our calls, unhinge our heads and open them? It's a good ambition, a god's ambition, to believe that it can know. The rest of us, so broken, have to take some of it on faith.

The skybound one that makes a droning sound the one who soars and, joysticked, streams information into a trailer in Nevada—the servered one the sometimes severed one when the control stream goes off-line and it is unleashed and finally on its own, all grown up and free in whatever way a machine can be, left to abide by its instructions, its trick heuristics, and so it feels *alive* for once, like the babysitter's zoning out downstairs and its parents haven't been seen in years, and—kickass!—it strikes a shelter and strikes again & somewhere else a video screen concatenates the blast with a dozen others, tags it, encodes it in its files.

Is there a god in that? What do we believe about what time can mean in a godless land where we impersonate minors online so as to lure them here for the NBC television show *To Catch a Predator*? I get that we love catching predators: even my daughter loves watching *Catching Monsters* (a show in which a Polish survivalist dude goes on a series of very dangerous hunts to catch monstrous aquatic beasts—though he doesn't kill them, thankfully: he releases them later; he's only in it for the chase, he explains). We don't catch enough predators in life, so we can at least hope our fiction does. But at the same time, if we are always trying to catch a predator, what does that make us?

I don't have that much sympathy for predators—particularly creeps trying to ensnare the underaged online—but there's something pornographic about watching someone try to catch them, too, to lure them into a trap in order to confront them on camera. Consider the case of Bill Conradt, one predator caught in an episode of *To Catch a Predator* in 2006. If you haven't seen it, the show works like this (according to an *Esquire* article on this particular episode):

> *Dateline* leases a house in a small town somewhere in America and wires it for sound and video. Members of Perverted Justice, a group to which *Dateline* pays a consulting fee, pose in online chat rooms as underage teens living in that small town. If an adult man starts hitting on one of these fake kids, the Perverted Justice decoys save the transcripts of his chats. Eventually, the man is invited over to the wired house for a liaison. When he arrives, Chris Hansen confronts him with a

printout of Perverted Justice's chat transcripts and attempts to interview him. As soon as he leaves the house, local cops (the Takedown Team) arrest him and charge him with online solicitation of a minor. Each episode focuses on a decoy house in a single city and documents the catching of six or seven men.

This one went a little differently. The *To Catch a Predator* team engaged Conradt in these chats with an actor impersonating a thirteen-year-old boy. They tried to lure Conradt to the decoy house for sex, and planned to confront him, but he wouldn't come. He stayed home instead. The camera crews and police liaisons staked out his house, hoping that he'd come out so that he could be confronted. He didn't, perhaps because as a criminal prosecutor he'd understood to some degree what the situation was. Or perhaps he'd seen the show? He likely saw the camera crews and vans and police subtly staking out his home. The neighbors did and wondered what was up. Spurred by the television team, the police eventually sent a SWAT team to break down the door to his house, and, cornered, he died by suicide.

So what god watched, and was it us, snacks tangled in its mandibles, as the body cooled gradually, degree by degree, until the god could no longer pick him up on infrared? What gods watched the episode later on television and felt a little more alive?

Payback Time

WHEN IN DOUBT, if you don't know how to feel watching a movie, listen to the music. It's your cue: here we hear the martial theme from earlier, but it's become a little more frantic. Before, the score was the sound of human (male, really) mastery, of effectiveness and domination. Here it turns with a touch of fear. It's urgent now. No longer, it suggests, is this team of badasses apex predators. Seeing them from above, we hear this shift in tone and think maybe these men are in more danger than we thought. The soundtrack to the men's moving through the forest is juxtaposed with the quieter, more contemplative soundtrack of the predator when we watch them through its POV. We hear what it hears too: its POV isn't only visual. We haven't *seen* it yet, but we've seen through it.

Before we get too uncomfortable with this creeping sense of vulnerability, though, the team gets to the guerrilla camp, and it's payback time, as Blain says. Payback for what exactly? Aren't *we* the invading force?

The guerrilla camp presents a plausible enemy and a familiar problem to solve—one I commonly encounter in first-person shooter games: how to kill them all without dying myself?

This being an action movie, it probably won't be the most elegant solution. Dutch sets a timed bomb in the back end of a truck, lifts the truck, and rolls it into the camp, where it blows up, and after that the team lays *waste* to the guerrilla camp. Guys get shot and explode and fly everywhere. This is the purest action-movie part of the action movie, a scene familiar to anyone who's seen movies like this. Explosions, lots of stunts and flying bodies, spraying machine gun fire, and here you'll find the movie's only actual one-liner ("Stick around," Dutch says, after throwing a giant knife into the chest of some guy). I guess you could count the line where Dutch kicks down a door and then says "Knock knock" as a one-liner, but it's so uninspired as to hardly merit mention. For better one-liner action, go to the aforementioned *Commando*. At one point, John Matrix, the improbably named character Schwarzenegger plays, dangles Sully, a minor bad guy, off a cliff in order to extract some information. When he returns to talk to the female lead, she asks, "What did you do with Sully?" He answers, "I let him go." Which is legitimately funny, even though it's at the expense of the life of a human being. I mean, a character.

What do these jokes do in these movies? By reducing a horrific act to a comic one they minimize the action we're watching. That's the nature of comedy. It redirects horror into absurdity. It digests a death in a breath. This is one of the things this movie—and its ilk—mean to say about masculinity. That's what masculinity is, and does: it minimizes or sublimates emotion. It puts up a skin between the soft part of the self and the hard facts of the world. Taken from another angle, this is a story about some low-level hired guns in the jungle who may well have families and wives and kids. They probably got hired to do a job, and maybe they shouldn't be doing the kind of job this is, but getting massacred by a bunch of overgunned Americans probably isn't fair recompense for that misstep.

Is this national security we're trying to achieve here? Who

knows? Who cares? Things are about to explode, which is why we're here. Dutch improvises, setting timed explosives in the back of a truck that's up on blocks. He lifts it—we see his ingenuity backed up by his strength—and I feel that good game feeling again. Satisfying first-person shooter games give you options for engaging conflict, which is where your subjectivity is engaged. Go in firing and attack the camp straight on? Use stealth and pick the bad guys off one by one? Or find another way? Dutch finds another way. The truck rolls toward a table with a bunch of guys (bad guys, we understand, so not really guys at all, or not the kind of guys we care about) eating lunch. It looks like they have beans and tortillas, which makes me hungry, watching it. Another guy walks in with a bowl of something. Blain sees the truck, says, "What the fuck?" Then the truck blows up, augmented with a "Nooooooooo!" Dillon says, "Showtime, kid," and the whole ballet of guns and death begins. Bodies burn. Bodies fly. People seem to die. Canisters of something flammable explode. Death rains down on the camp from our heavily armed heroes in the trees. Afraid, these unnamed characters shoot wildly in every direction as buildings burn behind them. The scene is filled with the cries of flying men, then the cries of burning men.

Amid the falling and the blowing up we are introduced to ol' painless, the movie's most unforgettable fetish object. Ol' painless is the insanely powerful minigun Blain totes, a colossal, hyper-fast-firing machine gun with a rotating barrel that destroys everything in its path. We'll talk more about ol' painless later, but for the moment just sit back and watch it go, since spectacle is its entire point: how it looks and what it does (or seems to do). Blain uses it to completely eviscerate a pair of hapless guerrillas. Not shot: they're nearly liquefied for our delight.

We hear a whining sound. Is it ol' painless? We can't yet place it, though it will eventually be clear it's a helicopter. Oddly, writing this I'm reminded that was the word I misspelled in the regional spelling bee in eighth grade (right around the time of *Predator*'s release) in one of the final rounds: *helicopter.* For some reason I spelled it *helicoptor.* I remember sounding it out in my mind on-stage, and it feeling not quite right but I couldn't think of any other way to spell it. And lo, I was eliminated. As the competition progressed I could have spelled all the rest of the words right, I thought to myself, even if that's just a convenient story about who I believed I was or could be.

While we're watching this action sequence, there's almost no time to think: wait, what exactly was watching the team as it moved through the jungle? This whole sequence occurs in our spectra, not in infrared, but the implication is that both we and it are watching the Americans kill nearly everyone in the camp. Are we impressed? Is it impressed, whatever it is? We are meant to be impressed. To marvel at their efficiency. To be happy to be on their side as everything explodes.

And now we see the chopper on-screen for the first time. Dillon shoots it up. Then Dutch blows it up. We see a stuntman burn and scream three times. There are nearly constant gunshot sounds. I realize watching this again that the only other sound we hear during almost the entirety of this sequence is the sound of screams, men muttering indistinctly, explosions, and rhythmic gunshots, which the more I listen the less I can distinguish them from the snare drums in the score. There's a slow-motion shot of two guys being thrown out of an exploding guard tower and into a convenient pool of water, followed by a rain of debris. That trailing rain is a fantastic touch, how it puts a period on the end of their death sentence after they hit the water.

Spare a thought for these stunt guys, they want me to pause the action to tell you:

We're thrown for your enjoyment: in pairs, in threes sometimes; rarely on our own. We all know that one man flying and on fire is not as good as two. It takes two to make the shot go right: the lead stunt flies; the understudy watches the body

go, learns how to coach the light to—barely—obscure his face.
Later we will compare our thoughts and trade positions.

Our pain is what merits your attention. Down here in the
"guerrilla camp", we weren't even the right guys to kill; we're
here to look lackluster and explodable. We're casualties, of
course, but our deaths are casual: our extinguishment is what
demonstrates effect. We die to show they matter. I mean, your
stars aren't only shooting nothing.

What if you knew they were shooting nothing? Later they
are shooting nothing. In one of the film's best scenes, your
protagonists unload their magazines into the jungle at crotch
level, leaving nothing standing, turning what was once an ecosystem into a clearing, preening in the smoke and light they've
made, and learning zero of their foe or of themselves.

Next they might as well install a mall and fill it with Orange
Juliuses, Jamba Juices, Wetzel's Pretzels, Hot Dogs on a Stick,
and other American shrapnel. Such are the godless scenes we've
made. Or if a god is here, it is probably the Predator, and through
him may we be redeemed by being skinned alive, our skulls pol-
ished for the trophy case. Or else the god's the camera that, by
the movie's end, presents to you the thing's strange face.

Some of us look better dying. Don't feel sad on our account:
our lives have meaning too. Our evenings are as full as yours,
if not fuller than the stars'. We long for lovers as far away from
here and dark and hard as stars, like the poem we once read
said. Instead we have each other: the stunned and blown-
apart; the menacing but shot; guerrilla soldier destroyed in
van; guerrilla soldier killed in tree; hostage executed by the
Russian; smoking guy who's strangled; oblivious guard; guerrilla overcurious about the sounds of unfamiliar birds, thus
stabbed; dudes eating lunch, exploded; tried to run, on fire, then
shot; badly burned, emoting briefly guerrilla soldier.

Confined to end the credits if we're credited at all, and found
there under Stunts, Additional Personnel, this is our talent

and our wage: to be blown up with grace, to receive our daily shower of grenades, to believe it is a blessing, to flail appropriately from elevated bunkers, towers, snipers' posts high up in trees: from here we oversaw your progress. From here we shot at you to no effect. What would it take to finally bring you down?

Dear protagonists, what do you know of pain? You inhabit it so briefly, en route to warmer stories. It's as if you're not alive at all.

To be or not to be the background for your simulated heroism: it's a choice, this way of living voicelessly. We know fire more intimately than you could ever know. From your chairs below you watch us fall and botch a take. The scream was a little out of sync. Have another drink and flex and grease your face. We'll have another go.

Do you believe you survive because you're clever? Those of us who know, we fallen few, will fall for you forever.

Of course, Dutch's gun is bigger than everyone's except for Blain's ol' painless. Even his binoculars are three times the size of Dillon's. This is a genre of film with a size fetish after all: the bigger of everything the better. Mac gets pinned down by another ineffectual guerrilla, and Blain blows the dude out of the tree. His body falls through the thatch roof of a building where Poncho and Hawkins do not seem remotely fazed at its arrival. Here's a passing shot of some boxes in the camp labeled, inscrutably, 6-507 FA and F.A.-1873. As if to say that's enough of gunshots alone, here the soundtrack comes back in to hasten things along. Billy shoots a wall and starts a fire. Blain blows apart another group against the background of some oil drums. As Dutch works through the camp a guerrilla tries to sneak up on him, only to be run through by Dutch's thrown knife, prompting the one-liner I mentioned earlier, and that's the last time we'll see the knife in this movie. Dutch kills some more guys, then he knocks out the movie's only female character with the butt of his gun. And this is how we're introduced to Anna, a guerrilla played by Elpidia Carrillo: silent, motionless, unconscious, her hair splayed out beneath her against a background of notes written on graph paper. Dutch says, in response, "Shit." Shit: Why? Because he doesn't know who she is? Because a woman has suddenly joined the picture?

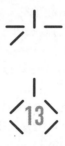

Rewind: A Nothing Shot

LET'S REWIND FOR A SECOND. At 25:26, here's a shot of a man backdropped by darkness, smoke, and fire, shooting toward the camera, his face obscured by the white burst of the muzzle flare. How to explain how I'm haunted by this nothing shot? If it weren't for the ability to still the film I wouldn't have ever encountered it. In it we see one of the guerrillas, or whatever they are, against a backdrop of fire, as his whole workplace, the whole encampment, burns. Our protagonists made this occur.

But in this one frame his face is light: a wash of white, a hole, an effect of the muzzle flash. Because of this I can imagine any-one's face behind it. It even looks a little like the hockey mask we make our Jasons wear so as to preserve their mystery.

Driving behind a van today I saw a Buffalo Bills NFL team helmet decal on the back window opposite what looked like a Jason mask. I mean, it was a hockey mask for sure, but the sort that Jason wears, and as a fan of hockey I was disturbed by how quickly I read it as a killer's, not a Sabre's. In passing the vehicle I saw the side window had another decal with a mask and a machete, captioned with *Protected By*, so there's intention for you.

What to do with the other decal, then? Did the driver love both serial killers and the Buffalo Bills? Does he simply like spectacle? Does he go for men in uniforms and masks? Or does he mean the Bills decal to obliquely call up Buffalo Bill in *Silence of the Lambs*? That seems like a stretch, but the way the display did not resolve was what captivated me.

Everyone's expendable, we're told a little later in the film, but that's not quite true. It's impossible to believe it of you.

I hold that thought as I pull out a chainsaw to dismantle the half-a-century-old forty-foot ocotillo that last week's monsoon storm took down. I think of my father and his Kevlar chaps and his frequent visits to emergency rooms after harming himself with tools. Maybe it's because he's been badly cut so often that it seems to me that, like a stuntman, he'll never die. But still I am my father's son, so I check myself while pushing hard and trying to cut through one last limb. I could press it further but I dial it back. I take a break. I've made myself bleed enough in other ways and have other things to do today besides the emergency room.

I don't believe the shot's intentional, and if it's a metaphor it's not their metaphor but mine. Finders keepers, and whoever smelt it dealt it: the man's no man but muzzle flash personified, a skin that holds an action, a blank shooting blanks, a container. If I look at it long enough I start to see myself with my finger on the trigger.

THE WHOLE CAMP APPEARS to be subdued (because they're all dead) except for one guy up in an elevated position. Poncho says to Blain, "You're hit. You're bleedin', man." Blain responds, "Ain't got time to bleed." Poncho fires some grenade rounds up in the air. He says back, "Oh. Okay. You got time to duck?" Indeed he does. We laugh, or we're supposed to, because what else are you supposed to do? Explosions ensue, and with that, the last guerrilla—aside from, I guess, Anna—is thus eliminated. The whole raid took approximately nine minutes of screen time.

OF COURSE I LOVE STUFF BLOWING UP. It's a couple of days after July Fourth and I blew up a bunch of fireworks this year as usual. I know people with dogs hate it, and I understand why, but I love it all unreservedly. What we blew up is nothing, though, compared to the professional-class stuff our neighbors a couple of blocks over blow up. Ours are all ground-based, basically a series of elaborate sparklers, spinners, and fountains. Theirs are the big-boom sky kind that you see in major fireworks displays, the sort you could *really* fuck yourself up with if you're not careful, the sort that as teenagers we *really* wanted but could not afford. I point this out to say that I will always watch things blowing up in life or on screen, but also that if you don't, stick around, since things get more interesting going forward in the movie. Remember that big-ass knife Schwarzenegger threw?

If you wade through the credits, you'll note that Jack W. Crain, Weatherford, Texas, is credited for "knife design/production." You can buy his patented predator machette (not to be confused with a banal one-*t* machete, the kind you'd buy just anywhere) for $1,945 from his website, these thirty years later. What do you get for the man who wants a trophy but doesn't want to kill and clean the spine himself? What do you get for a man who knows *that's* not a knife; *this* is a knife? What do you get for a man who wants a $1,945 knife, or who needs another knife? What do you get for our fathers, who art in heaven, hallowed be thy names? If $1,945 is beyond your means, Crain also sells somewhat cheaper models from the film and from the sequel. He made the knives for *Road House* too. Who knows how many more of these action films I've watched built scenes to show his knives? Collect all ten or you're a chump. It's almost as if capitalism is what drives the action! Is it important that we know to find Jack W. Crain in Weatherford, Texas, so as not to confuse him with the other knifemaking Jack W. Crains?

McTiernan mentions in the director's commentary that he didn't know how the knife got in the movie. He tells us Crain was hassling

the studio to buy his big dumb knives, and somehow the producers ended up buying one of them for Schwarzenegger in the
movie, but the thing was so heavy that while filming, they knew
they had to find a way to get rid of it. They settled on his throwing it in this scene, and they didn't have him pick it up afterward.
I love that fact: that the filmmakers were so burdened by this big
dumb knife they had to write it out as quickly as they could. This
also maybe explains the flaccidity of the joke.

SO WE'RE TWENTY-NINE MINUTES INTO THE FILM, and the action part of the action movie is mostly over. The big explosions
are almost all spent. That set piece must have burned through a
large portion of the budget. The carnival is over. We're taking down
the tents. And in the smoke and ruin, Dutch now realizes that he
and his team have been betrayed, set up by Dillon and brought in
to do a dirty job on false pretenses. As their vision of what they're
doing shifts, there's a confrontation between Dillon and Dutch I
will examine later, and another cut or two. Another minute passes,
and we see again through the Predator's POV. Unseen, it seems to
be listening to them, trying to process the language, or at least the
sounds of what these humans say. The creature has some kind of
sound-graph readout on the left side of the screen that fluctuates as
it analyzes the sound. It looks kind of like a spine.

   We see their heat signatures, the way they move, how their bodies
relate to one another.

   Mac kills a scorpion on Dillon's back with his combat knife.
Shows it to him. Dillon: "Thanks." Mac: "Anytime." The Predator
picks this up, this "thanks" and "anytime," both delivered in a tone
suggesting exactly the opposite.

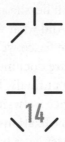

Extinction List

SINCE 1987, among many others, the following species have gone extinct:

In 1994, the Canarian oystercatcher

In 1994, the Javan tiger

In 2011, the eastern cougar

In 1994, the ivory-billed woodpecker

In 1996, the Zanzibar leopard

In 2014, the Acalypha wilderi

In 2004, the Mariana mallard

In 2013, the Formosan clouded leopard

In 1989, the golden toad of Costa Rica

In 2002, the vine Raiatea tree snail

In 1997, the Hainan ormosia

In 2004, the black-faced honeycreeper

In 2009, the Christmas Island pipistrelle

In 2008, the Caribbean monk seal

We're not extinct, not yet, as humans, but my daughter wonders about it. How long will it be, she asks me, until humans can't live in the world anymore? And what will we do then? She knows something about the climate fiasco we're heading toward, underscored no doubt by the nature documentaries she loves to watch, and has realized that we're animals, like everything else. Well, not like everything else, since we write novelizations and weird books about movies and novelizations and have a little more intelligence, at least on our better days, but still she's concerned, and rightly fuckin' so! We're APEX PREDATORS, we want everyone to know. These guys are the hardest of the hard core. The most American Americans! The best equipped! The strongest, fastest, and most prepared! And yet in the movie, however much we believe we're predators, we see that we too can be prey.

Hawkins, almost out of breath, finds time amid the smoking bodies and the destruction of the camp to make another dirty joke. I'm not sure if it's funny or it's not, but it serves to make Billy laugh. He's got quite a laugh, and we hear it in isolation and repeating. More importantly we see the Predator listening to the laugh. Is it trying to make some sense of it? Does humor register on an alien mind? Hawkins's joke does a lot of work for a stupid joke. We get an awkward delay between Hawkins explaining the joke and Billy getting it, in which we are the Predator as we try to make sense of human behavior. That delay allows us to feel the space between these guys, and between us and them, between me and men, and between the Predator and them. One senses in the Predator's attention the questions that I, too, have: What's a joke? What's its effect? What harm can it have? What use is it, evolutionarily? There is something at work that the creature doesn't see—that it cannot get from what it saw or heard—and that draws it (and us) closer.

Monette's novelization has its share of jokes too: I love how one of the guerrillas apparently on sentry duty is listening on headphones to music that we never get to hear in the movie. It's only after one of the team whistles like a bird that he notices and leans over to check it out and gets stabbed and killed (again—that's fucked up! Dude is only doing his job and gets stabbed and killed! If he wasn't such a noncharacter, we might care more). In the novelization, the song he's listening to is "Uptown Girl," by Billy Joel. And Monette tells us, "If the guerrillas had been alert they might have wondered what a blue jay from northern Minnesota was doing in the jungle. But they weren't alert."

Hawkins's joke also breaks the tension after the devastation of the guerrilla camp and helps us digest or at least turn away from all that senseless death. And then in the final scene in the sequence, Billy senses something—we don't know what it is, though Monette's novelization tells us that it's on account of his mystical connection to things beyond what's seen and seeable. He looks up toward the trees with his own answering question: wtf is out there? Here's how it's described:

> He was tapping another dimension now, the culmination of hundreds of years of inherited psychic sensitivity, Billy's birthright as the last of the shamans of his tribe. He had never been taught any of it. As he opened his mind now to vibrations from the unknown and unseen around him, as he zeroed in on the presence and drank its thoughts he was fully magic for the first time. What Schaefer had seen in him before was only a shadow of his transformation here. Billy had always ducked it in the past, or he shook it off like a dog shook water. Now he could not turn from it. He'd been waiting all his life to see as deep as this.
>
> He was cast adrift in his tribe's collective memory, suffused with legends and ancient battles. He began to sway as he murmured an old Sioux chant, and though he could never have told what the words meant he saw the image clearly. The legend described a Herculean adversary who had come from the meadow beyond the sky, a god-creature of wrath who had murdered half

of Billy's people. This was all a hundred generations ago. But the chant was very clear as it repeated over and over that the god-creature would return again. Billy quaked with fear as the chant locked in his throat. He could feel the breath of the ancient marauder, and the recognition sent shockwaves of horror through his soul.

Billy's eyes were wide and glassy now, as if he no longer needed them to see. Now he could focus directly on the alien's mind. He gathered all his strength till his ears rang with the beating of his blood. Now his own soul broke open like an extra-dimensional searchlight, and he scanned the jungle sky and intercepted the alien's thoughts, slicing into them like a laser.

Which . . . is just a teensy bit over the top, not to mention a trip into some mystical racist bullshit, but I do admire how this scene—in the novelization anyway—becomes an opportunity for transformation. One sees the poet—and the man in search of a subject or a story to transform him—working here to imagine, if not totally successfully. None of this is, however, in the movie scene, which takes exactly thirteen seconds.

We cut back out to a wider angle on the scene. There's Billy, looking up into the trees, surrounded by the total wreckage of the camp. Fire surrounds him. We see three bodies in the foreground, the bloody results of the attack. We do not care about these deaths at all.

WHEN I WAS THIRTEEN, of course, watching this film, I reveled in the destruction, though I wouldn't have been able to tell you why. The bigger the explosions, the better. The way the bodies flew was great. It made me want to blow something up. And we did blow things up. We blew lots of stuff up, my friends and my brother and I. Those years of my life were dominated by time spent with my friends doing dangerous things. I have almost no memory of parental oversight, my mother having died six years before, and my dad having remarried. I can understand now how difficult it must have been for him to raise two boys on his own. My brother and I didn't make it particularly easy, though we wouldn't *really* get into trouble until later. Well, my brother would never get into the kind of trouble I did, which speaks well for him in retrospect. My brother would be president of the senior class at the fancy school I got kicked out of and go on to Georgetown, then an MBA, and now he's an investment banker who likes to shoot guns a lot more than I do. We were collectively a lot to deal with then for my dad, and my stepmother, too, who was not well equipped for or apparently very interested in being a parent. My dad would turn to drinking heavily for a while, which probably didn't help anything, and became an angry drunk. I remember plates thrown against a wall and lots of words. I remember my brother and me blowing up and breaking into whatever we could find and running wild down by the Portage Canal in the stamp sand plain consisting of the mine tailings from the long-shut-down copper mine. What my father's life was like during this period I have no access to. Nor he, I suspect, to ours.

At the least, when I watch *Predator*, I feel safe. It all feels contained: all the anger and the devastation, all the destruction. It's violence, but it doesn't touch me. I laugh at it like I do a joke. Of course it cannot touch me. It's on the screen and I'm right here. When these guys blow up the camp it has no effect except in story. When the firework I'm trying to light goes off a second after it leaves my hand I still feel it in my hand for hours—and in my mind for far longer. My world, as I can understand it only later, consists of very many near misses that keep my life from flying wildly off the rails, like all those pedestrians in the action movie car chase scenes almost but not quite run down by a vehicle. The effect is almost like watching an action film. There are serious consequences, but often not to me, or not enough. I receive a series of glancing blows.

Consider: I spend a lot of time making homemade explosives based on recipes we find in places like *The Anarchist Cookbook*.

Sample articles include: "How to make nitroglycerin," "How to make mercury fulminate," "How to make blasting gelatin," "Formulas for the straight dynamite series," "How to make chloride of azode," "Formulas for ammonium nitrate compounds," "Formulas for gelatin dynamites," "How to make TNT," plastique, and so on. Elsewhere there are instructions on how to make Molotov cocktails, hand grenades, antipersonnel grenades, how to blow up bridges and make detonators and time delay devices, "converting a shotgun into a grenade launcher," "equipment set up for preparing tear gas," and a whole lot more. So we dutifully buy saltpeter from a local pharmacy, not realizing that its primary medicinal use is to blunt the sex drive, and have an awkward conversation with the pharmacist, who is wondering why we teenage boys are buying this. We try to make homemade napalm with Vaseline. We make Molotov cocktails and set fire to things, mostly intentionally.

When I later learned that *The Anarchist Cookbook* was written by a teenager, it did not surprise me at all, and not only for the shallowness of its political philosophy.

There is a violence in us—in all of us, but I suppose especially in me, as I seem to be around it a whole lot in my memories. I skip back five years before, to when we still lived in the farmhouse on US 41, so this must have been before or in the year after my mother died, and one of my friends and I are trying to skip rocks underneath cars as they drive past at sixty miles an hour. I couldn't tell you why. I would have been maybe six or seven. It's either my friend or I who skips one under a station wagon as it flies by, and all of a sudden it screeches to a halt. Backs up. The driver gets out—an adult male is all I remember, some screamy guy—and screams at us. He picks up my friend by the neck and screams some more. I remember watching him. I remember him screaming how he had his pregnant wife in the car. I'm sure we cried and apologized. He let us go, but I remember the intensity of his anger. Was that protection we were seeing or something else?

What would he have looked like on infrared? He let us go as he cooled down, maybe, or walked off in disgust. I wonder now what was he going to do? And assuming the story he told us was true, what was his pregnant wife thinking in the car, watching him pick up and nearly choke a six-year-old? Was this some new aspect of the man she had now witnessed? Or a premonition of what he might be like as a parent? I should admit here that I've let anger take me, too, as a parent, but not to the point of almost harming a kid—mine or anyone else's. And that feeling of being inside the anger is like being outside myself, or inside some other version of myself. I'm out of control. It doesn't happen often, thankfully. It's not the version of myself that I want my daughter to see.

Later that year, my mother would die of cancer. And a decade after that, my friend J would blow most of his hand off working on a homemade bomb. He had forgotten to ground himself while assembling it in order to dissipate the static electricity, and it ignited on his desk. The explosion barely missed castrating him. He would have to have a couple of toes removed and attached to the remaining hand so that he retained some functionality in it. He was a little more serious than I was in the tinkering-with-bombs direction, but not a *ton*. I thought then—and think now—that this could have quite easily been me with the blown-off and reassembled hand. He (I) could easily have died. His (my) body could have been the one in the foreground of the shot, lying still as I looked up into the trees, searching for some meaning, as our protagonists had some conversations.

We grew up in a small town in a remote part of Michigan's Upper Peninsula. This kind of stuff wasn't supposed to happen there. This kind of stuff always happened there.

ON-SCREEN, after pausing to assess the scene of the smoking and totally decimated "guerrilla camp" for one more second, Billy turns and runs into the jungle. And we switch back to the Predator's POV as it approaches the devastation, seeing the infrared signature of the bodies as they cool. This leads us to one of my very favorite scenes, in which here we are again, considering *something* from the Predator's POV.

The shot starts black. And then we see what looks like a heart coming out of darkness, a hacksaw or a severed hand in a pool floating for a while before, waterlogged, it slips beneath the surface. Especially watching it as slowly as I do, one frame at a time, we can stay in that space of not-quite-knowing-what-it-is that's so pleasurable. I've come to appreciate the moments in films and games where we're wandering around an alien or ruined space trying to understand where it is we are and what happened here. There's so much pleasure in not knowing; I hate the pull of narrative toward revelation.

What the hell *is* this thing? we wonder (as the alien does—and here we're one with the alien, no small accomplishment). In a moment the image will resolve into the familiar: outline of a scorpion, knifed and crushed beneath a boot, then picked up and considered as it cools in an alien hand.

The contemplation is the scary part: that the Predator *understands* anything beyond the scope of battle makes it sympathetic, sorta: it thinks, isn't just instinct; it tries to get our jokes, to figure out how we relate, not only disassembling the heart but its terminology: aorta, vena cava, artery, ventricle, cardiac vein. In Monette's novelization it gets obsessed with the human soul.

What we see in its long looking is our mortality: the Predator apprehending the scorpion's color disappearing, its armature breached, becoming furniture. Little silenced dynamo, you were and no more are, your form a clunky metaphor for predator-on-predator, how we live and prefer not to admit: it's us or everything, then nothing always follows. Your prehistoric progenitor, the man-sized sea scorpion, *Pterygotid eurypterid*, was demoted in 2014 from top predator to scavenger on account of how we reassessed its compound eyes' capabilities. At first it seemed bad-assed and supersweet, but now we theorize it likely hunted "soft-bodied, slower-moving prey," according to a paper published in *Biology Letters*: "One thing it would need is to be able to find the prey, to see it," which it could not, and perhaps as a result, like the list that began this chapter, it too is extinct.

We see what we want, don't we? Extrapolate a claw to a monster's gaping maw: terror is a better story—it sells more copies—it burns the toner in the copier—it crashes the copter in the jungle faster—than wishing on a bumbling, bottom-feeding, glorified prehistoric carp.

Dutch and Dillon, Poncho, Hawkins, Billy, Mac, and Blain: they're extinct, too, that exact draft of superman. In the not particularly well-lit museum of 1987 you can find all seven, preserved in action scene after action scene. The camera especially admires their mouths. All are killed and mounted in the last diorama you see before you leave. Look at how they preen and spit and leer and clean their blades and guns: it's a lot like life, as Depeche Mode says three years before.

Dutch survives because the camera loves him best, knows no one's his equal. He makes it to the chopper if not the sequel. Michigan Bell's call intercept recording features actress Jane Barbe, who died in 2003 and still speaks to those who know how to listen. The Progressive insurance company chose my friend Andy's voice to clone for their phone tree hell. He tells me it's on account of how little life it has.

AS THE CREATURE TRIES to assess what happened, we hear bits of recorded human voices: Hawkins and Mac and, mostly, Billy's echoing, disembodied laugh, then Mac's "anytime," which becomes like a totem in the movie. This is the first part we see of the Predator, seen through its own eyes: its claw-hand in the infrared, holding something we killed.

I can't get over it. This moment of contemplation is almost gentle, the thing holding the thing we killed in its hand.

This disorientation is at the heart of what holds me in this movie past a hundred viewings. We identify with the guys—particularly Dutch, who is after all our hero, and we know how to relate to heroes in movies, and especially in action films. But these guys are also so far beyond any of us watching it: they're bigger, tougher, stronger, more glistening, more glib, more beautiful. How could we possibly believe that we are them, or that they are us? Instead, we are offered the role of Predator and thrown outside ourselves. It's easy to forget how much of us is embedded in the things we watch, how closely a film can cut to a sensitivity we have. When we watch another culture's movies it's clear to us what we understand and what we don't.

WAIT: pause, rewind a few seconds.

I've been having this experience of having a still image up on a screen and perceiving it to move, almost like stereoscopes or Magic Eye. I'm paused at 34:29 in *Predator*, for instance. This is a split-screen shot. It's few seconds before the Predator picks up the dead scorpion. We're still in its heat vision as it scans across the mess these guys left behind, and some things we're able to make out: a body, for instance, cooling slowly. At 34:19 I see what I assume is meant to be a recently killed body but it looks like something else: the body of a dog, maybe, throat exposed, head stretched back. Dead. I linger on it, still unable to really ascertain what it's supposed to be. One of the pleasures of being in the creature's POV is that not everything resolves (or not for me). Some mysteries stay mysteries.

But this moment, at 34:29, we're seeing something. I don't know what it is. The Predator's sound graph thing is on the left, and on the right is a black shadow that I swear is in the shape of a man's face in a Freddy Krueger hat. There's a smear of red and white streaking into blue. The background's blue: the jungle ground, I think. The smear becomes an eye, and once I see it I can't unsee it. I have the shot in the background as I type, and I could swear that when I focus on this paragraph the shadow—the face in the hat—seems to grow. It grows very slightly: the feeling I have is of being pulled slowly into it, though when I focus on the still, nothing moves. What kind of movie is this anyway, to have so many moving secrets within it? Do all movies conceal this much meaning? Or am I seeing myself, staring at the screen?

Edit: as I look at the shot directly I see the shadow head growing slowly, taking over the rest of the shot. When I refocus my eyes, it hasn't moved, however. It's a horror movie trope I'm living here. This effect has been happening to me more often in the past year. Maybe the past couple of years. Maybe I never noticed it before, or maybe it's a defect growing in my mind.

I hit *play* and I see the mystery resolve: it's a crate or a bench or something wooden, the one Mac killed the scorpion on. It's satisfying to not know and then know. These infrared moments are explicitly and beautifully digital, then rendered in the analog medium of film.

Interacting with old digital technologies always moves me, whether it's watching what we thought the future or alien technology would look like in 1987, or whether it's the feeling of typing with a mechanical keyboard in 2021. A month ago I bought a new mechanical keyboard on a whim, having typed for a decade on one of the Mac superquiet, low-profile keyboards I'd forgotten that I'd become used to. Typing on those barely feels like anything. It barely sounds like anything. Compared to the mechanical keyboard and the way my typing creates this soundtrack of plastic and metallic clicks. It sounds a bit like the staccato gunfire in the guerrilla camp sequence. The keyboard looks and sounds almost exactly like my dad's work computer, an IBM PC I'd be left alone to mess around with when he took me to his office. Typing this sentence on it and thinking of its military sounds, I get the pleasant ASMR tingling of that throwback feeling, the kind I get whenever I see someone typing on a monochrome screen. The screen could be amber like the one my family had on our first dinky PC at home or like the more common green CRTs on Apple IIs, for instance, or on my old MS-DOS machines before I jumped to color, into CGA and then to EGA and then to VGA, each new technology bringing new levels of realism. All the new is great, but there's pleasure in the old.

A couple of years ago I bought a word-processing program I could use to replicate that monochrome effect and black out all the rest of the junk that Microsoft Word wants us to try to use in the menus and on the outskirts of our screens. All it gives me is green-on-black. Its effect is immediate and visceral: I'm back on one of the machines I built from parts and used to play or hack or write up until the point where I was arrested for hacking and computer crimes and forbidden to use computers for several years thereafter. This was the point around which my relationship with computers changed, when they became less like extensions of my body and more like tools. Writing this I'm aware that this is exactly how some people talk about their guns.

The terms of my probation included that I not use computers "except for good," whatever that meant, so I duly helped out a couple of community members (folks my parents knew, largely) working with databases or fixing their machines. Otherwise I didn't touch a computer for what felt like at least three or four years. I mean, I didn't touch one in the way I used to touch one. The way I used to touch machines was an intimacy I would never regain except in memory and fragments.

When my family moved to Riyadh I'd spend all night in front of screens, both because the sun there was punishingly hot and because I'd discovered a US government phone line in Riyadh I could dial into with my modem. It would relay me—like magic—to a system in Washington, DC, that I could dial out from to any American bulletin board system, which I did a lot. As Riyadh was seven hours ahead of East Coast time, if I wanted to chat with most American users I'd have to do it in the darkness. And in retrospect, I spent as much time as I could trying not to be exactly where I was.

One of the many fucked-up things about living in Riyadh was

the sense of being there and not being there at once. We were Americans, in Saudi Arabia thanks to the American government, so only sometimes subject to the strict local social and disciplinary codes. With a diplomatic passport I could bring in contraband, no problem, like a moneyed prince. Whatever we wanted to do privately was pretty much fine: don't ask, don't tell, like the subsequent American military policy toward homosexuality. I felt pretty much insulated—as an American but also as a boy—from the consequences of disobedience. Women were not then allowed to drive or to go out mostly uncovered. We'd heard of friends of friends—Saudi friends or third-country nationals or sometimes expats who had left the compound— who had been caned or whipped. It was risky, generally, to be alone off-compound. Homosexuality was then—and still is— punishable by fine, public whipping, beatings, vigilante attacks, chemical castrations, prison time (up to a life sentence), torture, and even death.

I remember one conversation in which my dad asked my brother and me if we wanted to go down to some public square to witness a beheading. I was a little interested, but even more horrified by the idea. I didn't go, and I don't think my brother or my dad went either. The invitation may have been my father's joke: I can't really imagine him wanting to expose his sons to that, or to take his sons to a beheading, but I can imagine him wanting to jolt us out of our Western sense of invulnerability. He had and still has an occasionally perverse and very dry sense of humor, set up by his relatively anodyne way of being in the world. You get comfortable and then he surprises you with something really absurd. My wife and I speculate about the possibility that my dad was CIA, which he does not admit, but I wouldn't rule it out.

Even if we didn't witness the beheadings, they were real, and they are ongoing. Public executions continue in the kingdom. You can find photographs and video online without a great deal of trouble. At least 134 people were beheaded and/or crucified in

2019 alone, including at least one who was arrested at an anti-government protest when he was sixteen, an article tells me.

I realize that it's easy to riff on the horrors of other countries' justice systems, so let's also be honest about what America does. My country also executed twenty-two people in 2019, including four men who were arrested for crimes committed at nineteen. I mean, at least we have a much more elaborate system of trials and appeals, but it's well established that these are fallible, if not quite as obviously fallible as Saudi Arabia's executions, which are carried out without trials that we would find credible by Western standards. There are no appeals. In America, executions are mostly conducted by lethal injection these days, though there were two electrocutions in 2019. Lethal injection adds a thin veneer of science and civilization to the procedure, but the end is as brutal, and often takes much longer. Nine of the 2019 executions were in Huntsville, Texas, where I played disc golf a few miles away on a prison-themed course named Shawshank.

Even if we didn't go to watch the public executions, we watched all kinds of executions happen in action movies. The spark that started the team's raid on the guerrilla camp in *Predator* a few minutes before is an execution, in which "The Russian" (so named in the credits) shoots a prisoner in the head. And on our televisions all kinds of other brutal mayhem happened to (usually) bad guys in the '80s, "Russians," who stood in as the objects of our fear.

DAYS IN RIYADH were something to be endured, not enjoyed—not all that different from the punishing Arizona summer, except we have a lot more greenery in Tucson. On those nights I'd be on my screen, what did my brother do? I don't remember. He didn't mostly stay up with me: my time in front of screens was largely time spent alone. Not alone, but with the machine. With it reacting to my commands. It was time spent exploring all its intricacies: what it could do or be made to do, what I could understand about the vulnerabilities of the system I had connected to, where the system operators were too lazy to change the default passwords, or to implement basic security procedures. This was time spent in my machine—this is what it felt like—like wearing the machine, like a robotic exoskeleton, almost. I would read William Gibson's *Neuromancer* later, and I could relate to what it felt like to be so in tune with the system I was operating that it felt like an extension of my skin. I still love that feeling, which comes most often in games, where I've been playing long enough that I've learned the commands and controls and mechanics. I no longer have to consciously hit a button or a combination to do a thing. I just do it. And I'm in the sweet spot there for a good long time in many games. (*Skyrim* was a great example of this experience, or, after, *Fallout 3*, but it goes all the way back to playing games like *Rogue* or *Larn* when I was much younger. Those games seem so basic they almost don't qualify as games in comparison with the simplest games on the Playstation 4, but they gave me the same effect, only more quickly, their controls being far less intricate.) It's like being in the golden hour in the men's bathroom on the fourth floor of the building at the University of Arizona where I work. It comes between 2:00 and 5:00 in the afternoon, depending on the angle of the sun, depending on the season. It's a feeling of mastery, of being briefly at home in something or someone, of feeling connected. I recognize that telling you this about the men's bathroom is probably particularly bizarre, but the light in there has the capacity to be fantastic, aside from all the rest of the things people do in the bathrooms. I won't stay there when it's occupied, obviously, for reasons of not wanting to seem like a creep, but I value the moments I get alone in there when the light comes in exactly right.

And I value those moments of mystery and discovery too. The whole first third of *Alien*. Or wandering around on some derelict ruin or space station in, say, *Mass Effect*. Just being there in a mysterious space, making some sense of some of what you're seeing, but by no means being able to understand it all. That's the space

I'm in when I'm the Predator's POV, at least some of the time, and I cherish it. As I said, I'd stay in that space forever. But this is an action movie, after all, and the grammar of these movies usually consists of great cavalcades of balletic violence punctuated by more contemplative (if that's the word) moments. When I was young, I watched these movies only for the action. Now I watch them for the silences.

In Riyadh, on base, my brother and I could watch any action movie we wanted, as far as I can tell. The Saudis censored Western media except that which came in via the military and found its way into the video library, which was basically every movie you would want, with a couple of years' delay. There was no one there to tell us we were too young to watch anything. We were in a foreign country where all media worth watching was banned. Our mail would come censored by the Saudi censors, who would Sharpie through any bit of flesh in any catalog or on magazine covers so that magazines would arrive completely blacked over. There was nothing you would want to watch on television. Some privileged few, we'd heard, had satellite dishes so could get all the good things from the West, but as for us, what we had was a lot of videotapes of American movies, smuggled in at one point or another, there for all the Americans to use as they so desired. So Ben and I watched them all. All the action movies. All the Steven Seagal (mostly bad). All the Dolph Lundgren (bad). All the Van Damme (mixed bag). All the Stallone (mixed bag). And, of course, all the Schwarzenegger (the highest form of art when in top form).

The more brutal the action, the more visceral the emotional response, and the more powerful and entertaining the movies seemed to me at the time, and the next movie would have to one-up the last or risk being entirely ignored. This remains a disturbing cycle of increasing violence and desensitization, and one I have to renegotiate every time I want to watch one of these action movies while I'm on the treadmill and my daughter walks into the room telling me about some new animal she read about on the verge of extinction.

If the price of entry to those open, almost contemplative silences in action movies I yearn for now, like the one with the Predator's trying to comprehend what these humans are actually doing and my trying to comprehend what the thing is that it's actually seeing, is these bloody gun battles, then that's okay by me. I mean, I love the guns and the explosions too. Seeing things blow up still makes me grin; it makes me twelve again. But the flipside is also true: those charged silences cannot last forever, at least not in movies. Eventually our capacity for wonder must be exhausted, ideally before we understand all there is to be understood, as in all great art, and we're jolted back into the necessities of plot.

One more aside before we jump back in, however: I'm looking at that screenshot again right now and it seems to keep on growing. Being aware of the effect—even writing it down here—does not seem to diminish it or allow it to resolve.

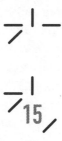

On Painlessness

AT 34:58, we return to our pilgrims' progress through the jungle. Blain is still toting a full load of ammo for ol' painless, and one wonders where he got it, as he's blown through literally thousands of rounds of ammunition in the thirty seconds we've seen it shooting. In real life the gun is inoperable as held by a human, even someone as beefy as Ventura. Though it's called a minigun, there's nothing mini about it: it's gigantic, and in its field form it has to be mounted on a vehicle (usually a helicopter). It shoots 6,000 rounds per minute (that's 100 rounds per second). Its magazine only holds 550 rounds, which would have been exhausted in less than six seconds, about the time it took you to read this sentence.

The prop gun was slowed to a bit less than quarter speed, 1,250 rounds per minute, so the camera could at least capture the sight of the barrels turning, and even at that speed it would have been impossible for a human to tote around and fire. Plus, the thing requires a sizable battery pack to operate, which is never shown in the movie. Some guys had to haul it around behind Ventura, which you can watch in some of the extras in some editions of the DVD. But this is, after all, a movie, and an action movie, so perhaps we forgive the exaggeration. And this particular exaggeration would be reprised in at least nineteen subsequent movies and forty-five video games, which also feature different versions of the minigun. The gun is another thing *Predator* introduced to us.

Ol' painless's name deserves some time, however. In a sense it may be accurate to call it that. The gun would nearly vaporize a human body in a matter of seconds. One imagines death would be remarkably swift, though whether painless or not is another question. Ask those who've been shot what it's like to have been shot, and you'll get a lot of different answers, from felt "like a wasp stinger was pushed into my skin" to "felt like a punch," "like a sudden impact of no sensation, then there was a horrible burning sensation," "felt like nothing," "like a weird wave of feeling hot and wet," "like absolute agony," "like a really weird bee sting," "like something blasted into me and was very noisy," "like a huge iron fist that goes right through you and comes back out," and "like a sledgehammer head . . . going through my midsection." "When you're in full on combat & don't have time to think about it, it's not that bad. But once things cool down and you're safe: man it hurts." I pulled these quotes from accounts I found online. You're not going to hear from anyone who's been shot with a minigun, however, as they are very unlikely to have survived the experience.

Calling the gun ol' painless is, of course, a joke, and it's a joke of a gun. You can't do anything but marvel at it. I clap my hands and squeal each time it comes on-screen: it's that great. Reality can fuck itself if we can watch something like this. Although the gun generates a ton of sound and fury, it signifies nearly nothing, really, against the Predator. It does speak to America and American film, though, and the way films like this portray death. If pain is reduced to a joke, the only deaths that matter in this movie—that cause any pain at all on most viewers—are the deaths of the team as they occur. I don't mourn—and neither do you—all the guerrillas killed by our guys earlier.

I TAKE A LITTLE SIDETRACK from the movie here to investigate the question of what ammunition ol' painless uses. The answer is, obviously, blanks, but: what kind of ammo does the gun that the prop ol' painless is portraying shoot in reality? That brings me to an article on Military.com, a site for "military members, veterans, and their families." While it's informational, the article sure seems to be effectively advertising the Dillon Aero M134D Minigun (its first line is "The Dillon M134D Gatling Gun is the finest small caliber, defense suppression weapon available," to give you an idea of what direction we're heading). The Dillon is an actual live gun, the helicopter- or jeep-mounted, present-tense sequel to ol' painless.

The embedded video is a live-fire demo of what the gun can do. It's 4:18 long, and the tone of it is not far off the shooting or the helicopter scenes in *Predator*. It takes me a while to recognize the song that soundtracks it. At first I thought it was an AC/DC ripoff: they couldn't have actually *got* AC/DC for this video, right? Wrong. It's "Shoot to Thrill," and the song does what the title says, and listening to it does, I admit, make me want to blow the shit out of a bunch of stuff in the desert, which, in the video, looks pretty similar to the Sonoran Desert, where I live. The guns appear to use tracer rounds since it'd be hard to show the actual trajectory of the fire otherwise. I wish I could say this doesn't affect me but it does, and if we place it side by side with the Predator scene, it reminds me again how odd a choice "Long Tall Sally" was for this movie. While gleeful, it could have clearly been something much more on the nose. The video is categorized on the website under "Video > Shock and Awe."

The homepage of Military.com is framed by a Geico ad, and its lead story is "One Killed, Another Injured in Shooting-Stabbing Incident at Camp Lejeune." The second lead story appears to be a straightforward description of Trump's bizarre 2020 graduation speech at West Point. A few tiles down there's "Why Soldiers Might Disobey an Order to Occupy US Cities," and then "Lawmakers

Move Once Again to Rescue A-10 Warthog from Retirement," referencing the ongoing internal battle in the military about whether
to mothball these old planes (they date back to 1972) in favor of
newer technology.

I'm familiar with this conflict. The A-10 is a close-air-support
plane, and most of them are centered in Tucson. I often recognize their distinctive profiles as they wheel across the cloudless
sky in pairs. That's partly because one of the games I played most
often in my adolescence was *A-10 Tank Killer*, one of the many
flight/battle simulators my friends and I played on our PCs growing up. The A-10 was my favorite because of how bizarrely bul-
bous the planes look, but also because of the sheer power of their
weapons. As a plane it is awkward and chunky but forceful, which
probably spoke to how I wanted to see myself at fourteen. I mean,
I also played *F-19 Stealth Fighter, Apache Strike, Chuck Yeager's Air
Combat, F-15 Strike Eagle, F-15 Strike Eagle II, After Burner, F-16
Combat Pilot, F-117A Stealth Fighter, Gunship, Harrier Combat
Simulator, MiG-29 Fulcrum,* and *LHX Attack Chopper,* to name
a few of the other war simulations that occupied my time. None
of these games use any ammunition at all (aside from Mountain
Dew), but some internet research tells me that because of *A-10
Tank Killer's* violence it was put on the index (of censored media)
in Germany by a federal agency, where it was made unavailable to
the public. I may have come to the game from a review in *Dragon*
magazine (five out of five stars), which I subscribed to and in fact
still have all of the issues in a box I recovered from my parents'
garage before I left Michigan.

Of all those flight simulators, I loved the two stealth fighter
games (*F-19* and *F-117A*) and *A-10 Tank Killer* most, but *A-10* most
viscerally.

It remains the closest to my heart, and when I see those actual
A-10s in the sky I take no small thrill. I've been in control of those
machines, even if virtually and with relatively shitty graphics, and
I've blown the shit out of Soviet tanks and probably a bunch of

so-called guerrillas. I killed God knows how many virtual dudes on hundreds of missions.

What did all that time I spent playing these combat flight simulators mean? For my friend Graham, who played probably the most with me, it led to a military career: after graduating from the Naval Academy, he joined the US Navy officers' corps. I ended up in Tucson, where I teach creative writing at one of the city's other top two employers and, evidently, watch *Predator* to exhaustion.

To answer our hanging question, the gun shoots 7.62x51mm NATO ammunition, each cartridge a little bit bigger than a AA battery. The minigun is virtually free of recoil, the website tells me.

WE ARE FULLY FORTY MINUTES into *Predator* when we finally get a look at the creature. Or we don't see it: instead, we get a look at its camouflaging shield. We see the outlines of a figure bending light to hide what's behind it. We see something, but we don't see what it is, and so the mystery is amplified. When it's still, it's invisible. When it moves, you can see there's something there.

According to McTiernan:

We had to in effect make a hole in the jungle, a hole in the background. . . . What I really wanted was a monkey. I had them make a red suit for a poor monkey. The problem was the monkey was so embarrassed by the red suit that he hid. He'd go up in the tree and cower, because he was too embarrassed by the suit.

They ended up having to use a guy, who put on the suit about the shape and size of the Predator suit. They made a hole in the background with the red suit and filled in the space with video of what was behind the suit, offset enough that we can see its outline. It, too, is an excellent effect, another one of the killer technical achievements of the movie that helps explain why it hit as hard as it did. When the Predator doesn't move, it's nearly invisible. Even when it does it's hard to see. You don't trust your eyes: something's moving: it's like the jungle's moving. Can't be, you say.

MY DAD SENDS ME a couple of boxes in the mail. He's cleaning out the garage, he says. He's got a bunch of my old stuff he thought maybe I'd want, including artifacts from my childhood: *The Bard's Tale* for MS-DOS, a game I played obsessively as a kid; some Dungeons & Dragons modules and maps; a photocopy of Charles Baxter's 1985 short story, "A Late Sunday Afternoon by the Huron" that I'd annotated in high school or maybe college; the copy-protection galaxy map from the DOS game *Starflight*; Predator action figure with shoulder cannon; and a copy of my juvenile arrest record. Collectively they comprise a kind of still life. I feel more than a little seen.

Like the alien, high up on a branch or like a cat in grass, sometimes if I stay unmoving for long enough I believe I can't be seen, but of course I can. Still is hard to be, but invisibility is maybe worth the effort. If you're a narrator you have to try to set yourself aside to let the scene proceed apace, to tell it clearly.

Besides, still's an impossibility. Baxter tries in 1985 to fix it all in time as did Seurat a century before. Both succeed—or neither does. Art's a bore. The world is too. It all stays in present tense no matter what we do. The determinists believe that if we had data enough and time, we could model it and still it like a game. In 1979 Richard Hugo would have called my father's box a triggering town; now that I've found it, I need to write the thing it triggers. It holds enough of my old stars to fix me in its constellation, if not to repair me. If art's a lie to tell the truth, how do we know what truth to tell?

The truth's a hell, says Predator: you're no more than the sum of what you kill and what you look like when you run. We had some simulated dungeon fun back then. We ran what labyrinths we could. I got caught, arrested by a Secret Service task force. One self stayed there—pinned for my transgressions against the banks, against the state.

Arrested for my explorations, I called Joe Cornell to ask him if he could make a wooden box to contain all my longing songs. And also, could he tell my dad that I was jailed and where to find me in 1987? Sure, he said, if it's intricate enough, but you'll have to call your dad yourself and explain the dungeon you're in. Also, I dunno why you would use your one phone call this way. And maybe you have other stuff to talk about?

Well, intricacy is not enough, or not intricacy alone. My life is fuller now. I still play games—expensive and sophisticated, with better physics, cooler sculpts, immersive scripts, and more compelling sprites, released by studios the size of which we'd never dreamed in 1985. Inevitability arrives inevitably. We're woozy with all of this muchness that we're offered. Does more detail make a better game or a more fulfilling life? Sometimes all you need's a name to bring to mind a world: *Rogue*, for instance; *The Bard's Tale*; *Adventure*; *Sentinel Worlds I: Future Magic*. A gesture or a word can conjure it. How the Predator's thermal vision can still find you when you believe you've disappeared.

Still, life with *Predator* continued much as it had before. I had no more insights into my condition. The derision I remembered at the hands of high school tools didn't leave me or lessen. At first I thought this was a lesson but it didn't smell like one. The mounds of rocks on the graves out back of my childhood home got no smaller or farther away. They still had nothing to tell me, like they always said they wouldn't.

BACK ON-SCREEN, wandering through the jungle to find a way out of this hole a few minutes later, Anna breaks away from Hawkins and runs. Hawkins pursues and catches her eventually. We watch them struggle in the Predator's heat-map POV, and it appears he's about to strike her. But when the shot switches to the regular visual the only thing we hear is him saying, "Please," trying to get her to stop resisting. The infrared shot is only two and a half seconds long, but I pause it there and go frame by frame so it takes longer. Even stilled, I get that movement effect again with the color patches seeming to spread the longer I look at it, and it's only when I let it play that I can tell again exactly what it is. Stilled, it's like a geographic map or a sonogram: is that one growing inside another's body or is it two? As I stare at its imprecisions—like the creature does, trying to make some sense of what exactly is transpiring—I find myself shifting into the creature's POV:

Don't be surprised. Killing's not so new. You try to stamp it out but won't. If none of you were killed you'd have overwhelmed your world by now, your species long extinct, a clutch of skulls and walls and Fossil watches, unused guns that glitter in the sun: from here they might as well be waffle irons or pitching wedges chucked in ditches for future archaeologists.

You can have your rules (every civilization does): permits for the season, which weapons you may and may not employ to exterminate a target. How many you can bag a season. What a season is. What you've deemed okay and not in war. You've even defined what war is and is not, though now you bend that definition with covert ops and drones.

Love, at least, you leave enough alone.

Because you are "tough on crime," nearly 1 percent of you are behind bars (one reason why we prefer to hunt Americans: you know the cruelty of form, what confinement means, you've long been toughened in your pens, and when at last released you go apeshit on Doritos; you marble nicely).

We the creatures hold these truths to be self-evident. We don't always drink beer but when we do we drink until our eyes are exes and we've been rendered sexless, comatose. Don't be morose. It's just biology, which we all know you failed. Opened up and fried, your brains are eggs in PSAs on drugs.

The roof's on fire, and luckily we don't need no water to extinguish it because it's dwindling on this planet. Soon you'll do anything for it except, apparently, conserve. Mr. Fudd, it's not yet fricasseeing rabbit season, nor will it will ever be. Instead, let's all sing and wait and see and let the motherfucker burn.

Back in our bodies now, watching their bodies fight, suddenly they pause—some calm is reached—and Anna turns her head, seeing something in her peripheral vision, then Hawkins turns, and we don't see Hawkins die but we see the effect of his death in the blood spray on Anna's face. She's in shock. We see the team running through the jungle and the camera's moving so fast to track their running that if I pause the shot again the foliage is green horizontal lines—it's gone expressionist—and then we cut back to the creature as it grabs Hawkins by the boot and drags him into the jungle where the thing and the meat that used to be a man disappear. The team arrives too late. Poncho follows a trail of blood from Anna's face, past the backpack, and comes upon his viscera, an unidentifiable pile of blood and intestinal coils. And now the film enters its second act and changes shape. It was a war movie; now it is a horror movie, and the writer's gone.

⟨16⟩

Mommy, Why Does Everybody Have a Bomb?

HERE I WANT TO PAUSE for a moment to consider time. In the long gap between *Predator* (1987) and *The Predator* (2018), we find 1999, the edge of one millennium and the beginning of the next, made famous in 1982 by Prince but mostly memorable because we became concerned that the way we had long encoded dates on computers (using only the last two digits, rendering 1999 as "99") might cause computers to understand "00," reached on 01.01.2000, as 1900, causing banks and power grids to fail.

Mostly it was okay in the USA that year, but the change did cause minor problems at three of fifty-one Japanese nuclear power plants. In the UK, 154 pregnant women were sent incorrect test results of the risk of Down syndrome, and at least two terminated their pregnancies based on that information. In *Predator 2* (1990), the alien spares a female detective because it can see she's pregnant.

Was it that year I began to move back and forth through time? In 1999 my mother had been dead for seventeen years. My daughter wouldn't be born for fourteen more.

With my car I hit a boar in rural Mississippi that year, which seems like a very Mississippi thing to do. I don't know whether it lived or died, or whether it was the last of its kind. That year is perched between the other animals I've hit: a bird (1992), a dog (1993), a deer (2012). I hope that list ends here. Often I rewind and replay those moments, on the kind of tape you'd still rent then, between when Blockbuster debuted (1985) and went bankrupt (2010), then dwindled down to its two remaining stores (2019): Bend, Oregon, and Morley, Western Australia. Though they still survive for now, the two remaining stores are not a mating pair.

In 1999 the global mean temperature was the fifth warmest on record. Nearly every year since has had a higher mean temperature. The alien in *Predator* comes only in the hottest years, so it's good we keep having more and more, a fact remarked on both in and by the fact of the sequels, which also number more and more. Predators attack only the armed; these days we are armed more and more (more than one gun per American in 2019). In 1999 we performed nine million background checks on gun purchases, mandated by the Brady Act of 1993 (named for the man shot and wounded in an attempted assassination of the president in 1981). In 1987 background checks did not exist. In 2016 they did; we did 27.5 million of them. In America, 28,874 people were killed by guns in the last year of the millennium. Of those 28,874 people (approximately four times the population of the town in Michigan where I grew up and where my mother died and my friend's sister was murdered and another friend blew off most of his hand), 57 percent were suicides, 37.5 percent were homicides, and 2.9 percent were unintentional. The remainder are ambiguous. In 2017, 39,773 died by guns in America, almost double the population of the largest city within a three-hour drive of my hometown.

In 2005 the Silver Jews told us, "Time is a game that only children play well," probably glossing Heraclitus (circa 500 BCE).

In 2002 Missy Elliott told us, "I put my thing down, flip it and reverse it."

The year 1999 is equidistant between Prince's first releasing "1999" in 1982 and his death in 2016, after which the song charted once again (all told it entered the Billboard Hot 100 four times: in 1982, 1983, 1999, and 2016).

If you reverse time some problems solve themselves. Global warming shrinks with the population. The *Predator* movies get better. We holster our guns. Bring them back to the store. Prince and David Berman and Laura Branigan and many others live again.

In 1998, Eels told us, "Thought that I'd forget all about the past / But it doesn't let me run too fast."

In 1999, the human population of the world surpassed six billion, give or take a few. That year the attempt to impeach Bill Clinton ended. One hundred forty-three people died in an Athens earthquake. More than 2,400 died in an earthquake in Taiwan. Fifteen died in Columbine, shot by two teenagers in a school, one of whom had been accepted to the University of Arizona, where I now teach, where I am now on the Active Shooter Response Training Committee.

Humans who died that year include Stanley Kubrick (director), Dusty Springfield (singer), and Iris Murdoch (novelist); Joe DiMaggio (baseball player), Wilt Chamberlain (basketball player), and Curtis Mayfield (musician); Gene Siskel (film critic), Dana Plato (actor), and Dylan Klebold (mass murderer).

In 2019 we are still looking for 1999: "Kansas authorities search for Adam Herrman boy last seen in 1999" (*NY Daily News*). "Montreal river searched for body of girl last seen in 1999" (CTV News). "Garden of woman last seen in 1999 excavated" (*Times* [UK]). "Digging to start in search for woman last seen in 1999" (BBC News). "Re-appeal for missing Hemel man last seen in 1999" (*Hemel Today*). "Pair on trial accused of murdering woman 'last seen in 1999'" (ITV News).

The West Nile virus was first seen in the United States in 1999. I nearly froze in record colds in Minnesota with my brother in an Isuzu Trooper II with a malfunctioning heater. We had borrowed it from my father. Gunmen opened fire on Shia Muslims in a mosque in Pakistan, killing at least sixteen. Unarmed Guinean immigrant Amadou Diallo was shot dead by cops in New York. We started using Napster. Pluto was still called a planet then. We still bought CDs then. A woman killed three at a shooting range in Finland. Rwandan Hutu rebels killed and dismembered eight tourists in Uganda. Two men became the first to circumnavigate the globe in a hot air balloon. I went on a first date with the woman who would become my wife in 2002. In 1999 the Dow closed above 10,000 for the first time. Two Swedish police officers were wounded by armed bank robbers, and later executed with their own service pistols in Malexander, Sweden.

In 2019 I listened to the album version of Prince's "1999," which is longer and much stranger than the familiar single version. It ends with a child's voice repeating, "Mommy, why does everybody have a bomb?"

A series of tornadoes featuring the fastest wind speed ever recorded on earth (302 mph) killed thirty-eight in Oklahoma in 1999. That year came between *Predator 2* (1990) and *Alien vs. Predator* (2004). My *AVP* T-shirt reads, "Whoever wins, we lose." (Not true.) That year uncountably many died. Some more were born. That year I turned twenty-four.

I DON'T REALLY KNOW how old Hawkins is supposed to be in the movie—he could be twenty-four—but now Hawkins is gone. Poncho interrogates Anna, and she says something back. Poncho translates her response as "the jungle came alive and took him." Dillon says, "bullshit, that's not what she said. What she said makes no sense." Translating the Spanish for myself now, I see she never says that the jungle came alive. She says the jungle took him. It's Poncho who adds the *came alive*. Neither of these things makes any sense, that the jungle took him or that the jungle came alive, and they seem about the same to me, so I don't know what Dillon's on about. The team is pissed and also surely scared. Dutch wants Hawkins's body found. They spread out. We follow them for a bit, with the martial soundtrack putting us on high alert. We feel anger more than fright: anger's easier to feel; I mean, it feels better to feel angry than to feel vulnerable, which is why we prefer to feel and act that way. Then as we track them through the jungle the camera pans slowly up the trees, as we hear the Predator's now-familiar theme music, and we see something black—or is it red?—dripping down a vine, and the shot goes on as the music rises, and we now know perfectly well what that red dripping is but the shot still goes on, drawing out the suspense. All in all we'll follow the blood trail for a full thirty seconds before we finally get the shot of the body, hanging upside down way up in the trees. This is another thing the team won't see.

Back on the ground, we turn to Blain, who had no time to bleed before, and follow him as he tracks something in the jungle. He hears something in the brush. We cut to another close-up of his gun as it takes up the entire screen. Shift back to his face: he says, "Come on in, you fuckers . . . ol' painless is waitin'." He puts his finger on the trigger. What's waiting is, uh, some kind of little mammal? The script tells me it's a tapir, but in the movie it's obviously not a tapir (no long snout). I look at the script one draft back, and this scene's not even in it, so that's no help. It doesn't matter what it is, I guess, because it's not what Blain's expecting, and he smiles and turns away, and as soon as he relaxes—and we relax—he's struck.

Time to Bleed

I GO FRAME-TO-FRAME NOW, watching Ventura move as Blain, and pause on the shot of him I love best. The shot catches a burst of light in the upper right corner as the Predator fires its shoulder cannon at him. Blain's been hit with something—we're not sure what. A spray of blood. The camera pans around to catch his face. This shot is right before he's hit the second time, before he's even aware he's been hit. The camera catches the light spreading out from behind him and covering the left half of his face. His mouth is open. His MTV shirt shows a stain of blood: his blood. He has only eight seconds left to live.

Here Ventura—playing Blain—is half man half light, which is to say an angel or a shade or a projectionist. Minotaur, maybe: abomination, blowhard, fool, weapon-toting sage, one-term governor, exactly the kind of politician I like as long as I didn't vote for him and only watch him from afar. He's my schadenfreude, fräulein, my big beautiful baby, and I don't mind saying that I'd spank him to stop him squealing. I zoom in on his face and can almost see through to whatever's shining from behind: the best evidence of God I got tonight (well, it's all I got tonight, so no biggie).

"Not God," he says. "Just ol' painless here, my big-boy gun. It's fun to fire. A spectacular. Look into the barrel of the lyre."

Now he's the Sibyl, mouth open to expectorate the beyond. In the film they turn to him for what passes in the jungle as wisdom. Mac loves him particularly. Bill Duke, the movie's strongest actor, plays Mac hard: he's not the star but sure gets a lot to do, like the razor scene. After Blain is gone, it's Mac's hand clenched on the trigger of the giant gun as, ammo used, the barrels spin and spin, and the forest falls away. There are a lot of scenes like this, their fingers on the trigger. The camera finds Mac's mouth and holds it often. Like a grieving spouse he laments the loss of Blain and is killed himself shortly after, as if to sing "How Do I Live?" and say this rhyming end is the wage of friendship or something else, beyond which why bother to live on? I'm bad at friendship. I wouldn't burn myself to summon up your ghost or sacrifice my moment with the alien to lament your loss. I need my confrontation the same as you. I missed the memo somewhere and though I have fun hair it goes nowhere—or everywhere too easily. I'm not intentional enough. I mention the unmentionable. Mistake one affection for another. Make the wrong joke about your mother.

Then it's like when the film strip sticks and melts and we remember where we are: not Central America, not Mexico, where it was filmed. Not a jungle anywhere unless you're really reading this in one. Not in 1987. We are who we were, if altered slightly, filled. It's not hard to tear a hole in all of it: an email tells me that a colleague has lost his wife and his daughter both within a week. How can that be borne? Maybe it cannot. So instead look up. Put this book down: it doesn't need you now. Others do. Like a predator I'll be watching you.

OTHER ASPECTS OF THIS SHOT I LOVE: the bloodstained tank top that reads *MTV* remains a brilliant piece of costuming; through it Blain becomes America, which becomes more and more a spectacle. I love the jungle background Day-Glo green and the way

Ventura's mouth is open like a portent, like a portal. Soon he'll go aortal, lasered through by the Predator's shoulder cannon and then he's bleeding out, but for this moment he seems to know something that no one else on earth can know: what it feels like to be that empty. We get it: he's a machine of a man playing a man-machine who has no time to bleed. Until now he's been unstoppable, man with gun and in the zone. Nothing of this earth could touch him. And it's not as if these guys have depth: they're muscle-thin, merely skin to project a film on so that you can't see the light come through and ruin the effect.

But we can see the light come through. You know the flashlight-on-the-hand trick, how it dazzled you when you were young. It still dazzles you. You show it to your kid. She's gleeful. It seems like opacity, you know, but nothing is. Paucity and silence can suggest depth, you're told by someone else trying to get you to shut up so as to be sexier in your hexagon, to seek the light and how it strikes you so you can win the game. You'd look good that way, you say, all lacquered up and half-obscured. You put the engine of your sex in the frame. All benjamins and bens, bennies and JonBenets, Hennepin and terrapin.

Here Blain's a lack, a little zero in the center of the frame. He's half shed his skin already, will be stripped of it not a couple minutes later, the thing we wrap ourselves in and take for granted, that we get wet and cut: What would we be without it? Is that why the creature takes our skin away, to remind us how soft we are? It's impossible to ever really grasp our softness until we do, like most things, in the rearview. Blain's a dazzle off there, mazel tov, like vintage David Hasselhoff, like some 1980s satellite signal singing out there in the dark beyond the atmosphere and beaming our Dire Straits to us.

God, we watch him and he knows we are watching him. It's almost as if he's being raptured or something, or has emptied himself out so much that he could be possessed, as if anything could fill him.

Blain—or Ventura playing him, which is of course something different, but let's be honest: this is America, so it's not *that* different—becomes mayor of Brooklyn Park, Minnesota, in 1991. In 1998 he runs for governor as a Reform Party candidate. Only sort of as a joke, my brother donates to his campaign. He gets a couple of T-shirts in return. We don't live in Minnesota, but our relatives do. It's fun to think about and watch from a couple of states away. Surely an actor and professional wrestler and former Rolling Stones bodyguard can't actually *be governor*, can he? Well, he's elected, and from a distance (typing this I'm soundtracking this montage with the Bette Midler song), it's hilarious to us. Holy shit: Blain is now a governor! To his credit, though known for guns and fun, Ventura does not pander to Minnesotan deer hunters, telling them in an interview there's no sport in hunting a creature that can't shoot back. The only real sport is hunting men, he suggests, only probably as a joke: "Until you've hunted man, you haven't hunted yet. . . . Because you need to hunt something that can shoot back at you to really classify yourself as a hunter." He's known for saying stuff other politicians won't, which becomes part of his brand. This is both a weakness and a strength.

I ask some of the Minnesotans I know if he was a good governor. What I hear back is mostly qualified yeses, or, well, we thought not at the time, but then came Trump, and you know, they trail off, dot dot dot. The consensus seems to be that he started out strong, brought some fresh ideas to the state, spent too much time fighting with both parties (neither of which was his) and the press, got some good things done, but seemed defeated by the role. Fighting politicians in St. Paul turns out to be more difficult than killing guerrillas in films. In 1999, still governor, he returns to wrestling as a guest referee and as a commentator for the failed American XFL football league, which draws much criticism. He remains an interesting dude, speaking out for the right for gays to marry, telling a story about a friend during his professional wrestling days who couldn't be with his partner of twenty years in the hospital when he got sick, since he was neither spouse nor next of kin, saying it was cruel and "where do we get off that the government should decide who you should fall in love with and marry?"

In the Goodwill parking lot on north First Avenue only a few miles from the Safeway where Loughner shot my congresswoman and several others with a Glock 19, which is a gun that does not appear in *Predator*, my WiFi-scanning laptop wonders about a signal, asking questions of the air here since this store doesn't have a network, or not a public one at any rate, and my hacker days are largely over. Like a teen, my machine will handshake with and enter into anything that is unsecured, but there is no signal anywhere.

I search the store's interior for a fragment of a packet but instead find this rad two-headed eagle sculpture: How could you, dear former owner, dispose of this? And what hand held you, hybrid, patriotic, anatomically improbable, and unflying beast of myth, and did it wither away and die with you in hand or tire of your company? Or you, four-inch Predator figurine: you look like you made it through a war that you didn't even know was happening. Perhaps you did.

Bleached-out sticker on a pole outside that lights up at night and clouds here uncover the desert beneath the one we knew before and oleander and palo verde rise through chain link fence unstoppably. *Chain* the wrong word, really—ziggurat of interlocking wires (the barbed-wire fence that tamed the west was also used for telephone in some rural areas) and plastic strips threaded through the gaps so as to give off an impression of opacity and the world becomes transparent when we expect it not to be and we might buy guns at USA PAWN & Jewelry Co. down the block to commemorate in our own fucked-up way the six killed a year ago this day, two miles away at a Tucson Safeway, eighth of January and in that way the moment can be opened in an essay and if we might find out what is held inside it safely then we could understand it or understand ourselves and who we are and were and file it away under *invulnerability* and what is there to know about our days spent running along the dry river feeling tough, lost in thought or space beyond, anyway?

On the radio: "Every Day Is Like Sunday" and it is Sunday, a day for memory and we have our ears to car radios trying, like Cocteau's Orpheus, to tune in to some beyond: any would do. Each hour we encode anew and dispose of an older, other hour's accumulated living. In doing this we perform our dying. Remember: everything's a passageway to everything: kill a Predator and you've proved that you deserve another. They will keep coming back. Storm drains are underneath the streets—though driving forty-five, a bit beyond the posted speed limit so as to feel alive again like we live above the law or saw Steven Seagal lay it down for us in a grimace on a screen, we don't feel or hear the manhole clatter under tire but in the drains each strike reverberates throughout the system like a trilling telephone in a high school abandoned for summer or forever. If I could pick it up I would.

On the anniversary there's talk of healing in the wake of tragedy and what meaning can be made of a head-shot congresswoman's silent year or our years of wail and border wall and the way an interaction as simple as a cab ride can stain a life without intention. "Driver Who Took Loughner to Safeway Breaks Silence," says KVOA. "I took him there. And I mean that was it, he was perfectly normal, nothing strange about him . . . gave him the change and I left, and I guess right after I left was when he did it. No indication at all, like he was perfectly calm. . . . There are lunatics out there, obviously. Not much we can do about it though, but put them away."

We put them away in memory, barely, or etch on the B side of death in late-night mammary dreams, like remembrances of sexy statuaries that used to turn us on when we were teens, when anything could turn us on: a button unbuttoning accidentally or a machine bringing our ASCII screens to life. Now there's signal almost everywhere for those of us equipped to hear and interpret it.

It's a problem, actually, one reason why we need to keep the poets fed, since Cocteau knows they hear things the rest of us do not. Albert Goldbarth told me even starlight signals something dying, not shining. Even my machine's cooling fan is sighing something, trying to tell me something, make some signal out of static, maybe talk me down from my mortal panic, as if to say, why are you so far out and here alone?

BLAIN IS BIG and Blain is loud and Blain is mouthy and Blain is unruly and Blain is us.

And just like that, with one more blast from an alien's cannon, Blain is also gone, or at least the part of Blain that made Blain, Blain—not only the body of Blain, or the body of Jesse "The Body" Ventura—is gone, or quickly going. No one quite knows how long it takes for the consciousness to fade from a body after mortal shock, but it's probably immediate, and how quickly all that makes us us drains away or shifts to whatever's next, if you believe in that sort of thing. Will there be pain for him wherever he has gone?

Ol' painless, the gun that had to be artificially lightened for Blain to carry for our enjoyment, serves him no more.

TWENTY SECONDS LATER, at 47:30, we arrive at what is probably the movie's most famous scene. It was not in the original script. After Blain is killed, his friend Mac looks around to see whodunit, sees the outline of the alien, and, enraged and incredulous, begins firing wildly into the jungle. He exhausts the clip on his weapon, bends down to pick up ol' painless, and, having escalated things, thus begins mowing down everything in his path. Dutch sees him shooting and joins in. Poncho next, with a machine gun in one hand and his grenade launcher in the other. Then Billy joins the team and we see the guys lined up, guns right above crotch level, blasting into the jungle. Then Dillon shooting, too, then Anna cowering, her hands covering her ears. They switch clips, keep firing.

Tree trunks explode. Vines get shredded. There's smoke every-where. All of them fire blindly at whatever. Grenades get launched. A lot of foliage is utterly destroyed.

The team uses all of their guns in this scene, including the AR-15 assault rifle, the Mossberg 500 shotgun, the M134 minigun, an M60E3 machine gun with a shortened barrel, the Heckler & Koch MP5A3 (actually portrayed by an HK94A3), an M203 gre-nade launcher, a custom-built grenade launcher composed of an AN/M5 Pyrotechnic Discharger and a Heckler & Koch HK94, a Walther PP handgun, the IMI Desert Eagle Mark I (.44 or .357 Magnum), and the M1911A1. Enthusiasts may have recognized these guns on-screen, but for most of us the movie is an awesome advertisement for them. Like Crain's big knife, these guns be-came objects of desire for me and who knows how many other millions of men and boys. When I verify the list on the Internet Movie Firearms Database, a surprisingly accurate and exhaus-tive fan site that rips off the look of Wikipedia and is devoted purely to cataloging guns and their variants in films, I'm adver-tised to by Ammo Shop Online, Guns.com ("Hot Gun Summer: All firearms ship free"), Ruger (a handgun manufacturer), Case (a knife manufacturer), a twenty-minute video on the Smith & Wesson Performance Center Shield Plus (a cool-looking hand-gun), Springfield Armory Hellcat RDP ("the highest capacity micro 9mm in the world"), and "Raid Shadow Legends," which is, I think, some kind of freemium game. I'm not clicking on it for obvious reasons, but the language in the ad tells me, "If You're Over 50—This Game Is A Must!" meaning . . . what exactly? The ad features an attractive blond, seen from behind (naturally) in a prone position on a grassy bluff, peering through the scope of some kind of machine gun into a mist coming off a small lake. It's a weird ad, and when I enlarge it on my screen it gets weirder. On closer look, the woman is wearing some kind of fur-lined, metal-spiked shoulder pads on top of a sexy short copper tunic, so that's an odd collision of medievalish fantasy and first-person shooter, and obviously we're supposed to be looking at her ass, and so I do as I've been trained, but when I enlarge the image even further, it appears that where the tunic rides up and we'd see her thighs what we see instead is either fur (is she an animal? Her bare arms suggest the opposite) or grass (or is she vegetable?). It's superweird and getting weirder, and I've stared at it now for more than a minute, scouring it for meaning, and I have to bail out of this lacuna before I give them all of my personal information.

This scene in which the team shoots and shoots and shoots goes for one minute and seventeen seconds. That would be approximately 7,700 rounds fired by the gun that ol' painless pretends to be. The barrel life of the newest version of the gun is 200,000 rounds. This is a long time to only be firing on a screen. Hold this scene against the earlier trashing of the guerrilla camp: that was a montage of different bits, punctuated by jokes, bad guys flying, helicopters, explosions, stunts and stunts and stunts, hundreds of guys getting killed in different ways, all set to sheets of overlapping gunfire sounds. Standard action-movie stuff. This is intense, concentrated: seventy-seven seconds of straight-up only shooting, a total blistering spectacle. It wasn't like anything else I had ever seen.

The shooting only ends when the minigun's ammunition runs dry. We get a close-up of Mac's hand locked on the trigger, the barrels rotating, empty against the whine of the machine as it keeps trying to fire, even if it's empty. His fingers release the trigger. This devastation is followed by twenty seconds of total silence as the smoke clears a little.

The novelization describes it thus: "The blinding chaos was followed by the stunned silence of aftershock, as if the whole world had paused for a breath of grief."

18

Dear Paul,

Later, during the midnight dose, everything was peaceful as I gave him pills and made him drink lemonade. Then I watched over him till four, working on Predator *while I sat by his bed.*

—PAUL MONETTE, BORROWED TIME: AN AIDS MEMOIR

DEAR PAUL, so far I've used you as a kind of foil. Here you are, the backstory I use to legitimize my interest in watching men hulk, glisten, and blow stuff up on-screen: How funny that a famous gay poet wrote the novelization of the big dumb movie! Funny, yes, but that doesn't make it unserious. A tool's a tool. Reading *Borrowed Time*, your memoir of your partner Rog's dying of AIDS, and now reading your journals in your archived papers at UCLA—all that's left of you outside of those you knew—and even walking by the hospital where Rog died, I could feel my joke getting rapidly less funny. It was a shitty role I cast you in. I apologize.

Reading your handwritten journals in the archive changed my relationship with your work. These were sheets of paper we both had touched, almost thirty years apart. It wasn't always easy: trying to parse the handwriting and crossed-out words in one of your last poem drafts, "Xmas '91," that ends "here in the winter harbor of our last stand," and seeing the blank pages before and after, my breath caught a little, and then it kept on doing what breath does, thankfully.

The idea that, as the love of your life was dying, you were still working, a little anyhow, but *working*, on what you termed the ridiculous "novelization for *Predator*, the upcoming Schwarzenegger opus" must have become harder and harder to swallow. Or maybe it was the only kind of work you could do so that you wouldn't be left with too much time to feel or think or bleed.

As you describe the end of Rog's life, and the horrifying national silence surrounding the AIDS epidemic, I feel a burn. I knew this story only at a slant and after the fact. For (straight) boys like me where I'm from, these stories were not ones we got to know. Until now, I guess. Decades don't dull a story: it still affects me. This is a testament to you. I've come to share the growing sense of rage that led you to the point where you didn't even want to talk to those who didn't have a positive diagnosis, because what could they know?

I mean to say I found it harder to read your novelization as what it was or to use it as I had. The story seemed to multiply. All these resonances appeared: in *Borrowed Time*, "You force yourself not to think about the pain, where it hurt this time and how bad. . . . I went to bed certain he'd be responding to the drug within a few hours. I would not see the dying" and in the novelization and the movie, "I ain't got time to bleed."

I know you didn't write the script, but I'm beginning to see more of what you saw in it.

The journals show you watched a lot of action and war films. You and Rog both loved *The Terminator*, for instance (me too), and you'd written the novelizations for *Nosferatu* and *Scarface* already, so the language of men and film was not new to you.

And even if *Predator* isn't explicitly a Vietnam movie, it's been critically read that way. So it is a Vietnam movie, and it's not. It is an AIDS movie, and it's not. At no point do our governors see themselves or what it is they do.

Dear Paul, you watched *Platoon* and wrote of it: "*Platoon* was okay. Vietnam wasn't as bad as AIDS, or I don't care as much."

It's hard for me to shake the analogues to what you were writing and what you were living: in both, our protagonists are pursued, at different rates, by an invisible and seemingly unstoppable, technologically superior foe. Both are stories of mostly men surrounded by mostly other men, mostly under duress, dressed and undressed, with little time to bleed until bleeding's all you do. Both stories sport the language of battle (almost all death-by-illness narratives do, which always felt to me unimaginative, this retrospective narrativizing, but I see why we do it: it's a better role to die a hero than just to die). In both our protagonists are warriors, and in both they lose much, though not quite everything, not yet.

Go back to a line in one of your later poems: "the winter harbor of our last stand." Did you pull that phrase from years of watching films? How long had they echoed in you? What did it do to you and Rog, watching *Platoon* or *The Terminator*? What did it do to you, writing *Predator*? Did these things operate on you the way they operated on me then—or how they operate on me now, some thirty years later?

What does it mean to be thought of as expendable, like Dutch's men, to be sent in to do a different job than you were told you'd have to do, to know that whatever you accomplished there, it would never be attributed to you? That the war of which you were a part would not even be given the honor of a name by our government?

Here you write, from *Predator*:

As if he still didn't realize, even with the evidence bleeding all over the matted ground, just how very alone they were. . . . And twined through it all like the grip of a vine in a cotton- wood tree was the certainty of death—their mates', their enemy's, their own. A match had been lit deep in the mine, and the fuel that would feed the fire might turn out to be the whole dark earth itself.

After Rog dies, your journals start to cite survivor guilt, as does your memoir. Why was it *he* who was taken? Why is it *you* who is left? What does that mean? *Does* that mean? Could you have done more? "You start to think if only there were fewer errands to the apartment building, if only I'd picked up the Wednesday meeting, he wouldn't have gotten so run down. Maybe he would've been able to hold it back another two months. That way madness lies. . . . Then darkness falls and you're lost."

19

We Hit Nothing

AFTER ALL THE SHOOTING and mowing down the jungle, at 49:55 what scares the guys is not that the creature can kill them, though obviously it can, but that they—in spite of all their considerable firepower directed into the jungle—cannot kill it. They didn't even *hit* it (they think). What kind of thing *is* this that cannot be shot or stopped with all our many, many guns? And if our guns won't do it, what could ever do it? Fuck!

Even in death, we notice, Blain has no time to bleed. His wounds are cauterized and fused, as Dillon notes. All we have are questions: What kind of creature is capable of that? It's like it's not even American!

Having hit nothing, the crew digs in as darkness falls in the jungle. They make their camp and mine the perimeter "with everything we've got."

And after all that expenditure of ammunition and anger, we pause, and here we finally have time to bleed: a little anyhow. The film gives *us* space to feel some emotion, even if the characters almost never admit it. We insert our feelings into that space. Good art makes room for this.

Seeing Mac broken up, Dutch tells him, "He was a good soldier." That is the breadth of emotional response allowed, it seems, in a scene like this between men like these. (No one says anything about Hawkins. If anyone would have, it would be Billy, the recipient of his jokes, and Billy isn't saying anything.)

But it's clearly not enough. Mac responds, "He was, uh, my friend."

This is true, at least. Blain and Mac's relationship feels like the most real one in the film. That's one more real relationship than in nearly all action movies of the era, in which the relationships between characters rarely feel more than a convenience of the plot.

Mac turns and disappears into the jungle. Dutch stares off into the darkness. In what feels like a continuity speed bump, that dark scene cuts into one with more daylight, with Mac grieving his fallen friend. The music echoes (or perhaps is, I think; I'm not sure) "Taps." Mac pulls back the shroud covering Blain's body and stares at him, or the body where he used to be. He takes a swig and places the flask they shared on Blain's chest almost as a benediction. He says, "Good-bye, Bro," and then the moment is over.

PREDATOR IS BOTH about and a catalyst for male connection. It's a shared point of reference for many of my friends, which is why we all quote it, or when someone else quotes it we quote it back. This is how we talk to one another, when we talk to one another. I mean, it's not the only way we talk to one another, but it's a sure winner when someone brings it up, a shared reference point and a site of our own emotional investment that when invoked enough times becomes kind of a bond. I suppose any big shared cultural reference works like this, and that is part of what makes this film awesome and keeps it awesome, all these references feeding back into the loop that keeps *Predator* alive for me.

And it's not only the movie either, but also the whole massively expanding franchise and imaginative universe that *Predator* has spilled out into with all its versuses and all its sequels and novel-

izations and novels and video games and everything. We all want
to test ourselves against the Predator, which is why we can play
against it in a *Call of Duty* expansion, one friend tells me, or *as*
it *or* against it in *Aliens vs. Predator* on the Atari Jaguar that my
friends and I played obsessively for a summer or two. I'm sure it's
why I can use it as a Snapchat filter that I run occasionally in one
of the many Zooms I've been on in the past twelve months.

Predator isn't only media but an online ecosystem: there's a very
active community of *Predator* enthusiasts and cosplayers, many of
whom gather on the "Predatorium," the user forum at The Hunter's
Lair, a website where hobbyists gather to discuss the intricacies
of building believable alien dreadlocks and how to properly craft
your own shoulder cannon. One of the threads I like the best in
the Predatorium is a list of all the names humans have come up
with for their *Yautja*, the term the later novels in the series coin for
the Predators. All the deep enthusiasts use this term. You might
not think all of their Yautja have names, but you'd be wrong. Why
create and play a thing if you can't name it? So I come to the users'
names with a ferocious glee:

— Guan-thwei which means "Night Blood."
— I'm Spearaizer (still deciding last name) of Clan Scar.
— Kh'laz, Guharak, Zh'bat, Ahzhi. Mh'az the Unfavored,
   Sci'zi Redblade, Ourgha of Clan Tzuhrak.
— My pred is called Percy.
— Bak'ub, Straight Spear; "spear" is the way some pronounce
   my real-life last name. First name is Ei'luj, which is my
   first name that has been Pred-ized & mirror-imaged.
— A'kisha meaning: Little Demon Eyes.
— Ghey'Ihn'Mai'Ahz.
— Fluffybumblenuts.
— Nai'luj Wag'laman "Swiping Bear Claw" Elder of Clan Garo.
— I HAVE to name everything. I even name my weapons.
   My name is Half-Knife.

If wonder is what we're after, there is plenty here. The kind of lore they're building reminds me of my days playing D&D. The most serious build their suits from scratch. They trade materials and props and hand-painting tips to make their costumes pop. The word *costume* undersells the seriousness, of course. These second skins can cost upward of $3,000, not including construction time. On this forum, users share fan art, sell their sculpts, complain about the chumps who come here looking to rent a costume for a party. Here, too, they discuss desire: users ask each other (this is an actual thread), "What are you lookin for in a Predator?" (One answer: "I want to see convincing Predators, NOT PEOPLE.") I come across an intricate discussion of how best to make the alien's mandible clicking sound with your mouth, which I practice yet cannot master. The users go deep on language and mythology, and slag the sequels, or some of them at least. Most of these users are men, and deep in the Predatorium you don't find the toxicity you see in the YouTube comments on the Predator videos, for instance. These are the true believers. They're not interested in discussing masculinity or sexuality at all, mostly. Having fully bought into the mythology and fanworld of all things Yautja, they have less to prove about how much of a man they are. So they're having them some fun tonight. And it's totally fun to be part of this group. Their enthusiasm for the world is infectious.

I love watching people get AMPED about the quality of their sculpts on internet forums. They continue to call the roll:

— They'De—means "death, kill" . . . So far I haven't came up with a proper name for the clan she belongs to . . . just the symbol of it.
— Crazy Hunter because I'm a little crazy as far as the outfit of the Predator weapons and clothing, many of which have what others have not, or simply enter the crazy one indeed see later on my costume is

— My name is Uratz totally the class clown of the Hunting
   School.
— Every body calls me BraveBlood or YeyiThwei in yautja.
— Fuckface aka "Francis."
— A dark, bad-blooded Predator. The locals named him
   "Armagedo."
— My preds name is Vor'mekta Lar'ja which means "stalker
   of the dark" and I'm of the shadow clan.
— Name: Nuori / Gender: female / Status: Youngblood.
— I need help in thinking of a name for my predator/human
   hybrid any suggestions?
— I like the name Frayha but I am open minded.

I am open-minded too. Because I want to know what it means
to put on the mask, I bought a cheapie one online, the kind I'd be
mocked for on the Predatorium because I didn't make it.

Donning it is instruction in the other. It's hot and huge; it
weighs a lot; it must have been made to size, for a seven-footer's
head. I put it on and can't even see out of the eye holes. So I go into
a local costume shop attached to a dinner theater and ask for suggestions for how to modify the mask to fit me better. The woman
working there is clearly entertained, and suggests I get a bunch
of foam. It must be such a newbie question I'm asking, but I'm
not particularly handy tweaking costumes. I say thanks, and head
back home to figure out what I have. I could go to Hobby Lobby,
I guess, but fuck those assholes. Instead, I realize I have about a
dozen cowboy hats I bought secondhand, hoping to find one that
didn't make me look like a fool and was comfortable enough to
keep the Tucson sun off me. I wear few of them ever, so I decide to
cut the brim off one of them and wedge it inside the mask to get
it propped up. I can see out of the eye holes, but it also makes the
whole thing bulkier.

When I put the mask it on it's something else, I find: a little shell
I curl in to separate me from the world. I take mine to a conference

in Washington, DC. At conferences you're always wearing some kind of mask, even if it's not a plastic one, and I figure, fuck it, why not take this thing along? I'm not prepared for the level of delight I see in others when I wear it on the street, and to order a frappuccino at Starbucks. Guys always light up when they see me come: Fuck yeah, dude! Predator, dude! Check out that Predator mask! Hey, player! I hear. Player! White boy! One guy yells. I'm well past him before I figure out he's talking to me: I'm the player. I'm the white boy.

I think a little bit about some of my other costumes. Because my wife sells vintage clothes, we spent (before the pandemic hit) a lot of time at Goodwills, Salvation Armys, Value Villages, St. Vincent de Pauls, and other thrift stores. There are a lot of them in Tucson. When we first moved here, I found an adult tiger costume. Maybe it's a Tigger costume: I can't quite tell. I had to buy it. Who wouldn't buy this thing? It was glorious! When I took it to the checkout the woman at the counter told me, oh man, it's too bad you weren't here an hour ago. There was a matching child's tiger costume, and a kid with her dad *really* wanted both. He only bought the child's tiger costume.

I found this sad. At this point I wasn't a parent, but the thought that the dad wouldn't buy the matching outfit to dress up with his daughter depressed me something fierce. Come on, guy! I bought it anyway. I wear it occasionally, sometimes to teach in or give readings in. I was making some videos wearing the costume for a while. I ran a Turkey Trot in it one year. This was more rewarding than expected: people flipped out for it. I mean, in part it's a lot easier to cheer for someone in a costume than it is to cheer for some rando in running shorts. So I was high-fiving all kinds of people. The race was a blast, even if it was really hot to run in it: though it's a Turkey Trot (run on Thanksgiving morning), weather in Tucson is not typically all that cool in November, and I am a not unsweaty runner and a person of larger than average size. Also I had to hold its wiry tail—I mean my wiry tail—to keep it from falling off or whacking or tripping other runners. I would solve this problem with a safety pin the following year: I run in it every year now.

I keep hoping while wearing it I'm going to run into that kid whose dad bought the kid's tiger costume, but of course that kid would now be way too old for it.

After my daughter was born, I would wish that I'd have got there before that kid to buy the matching costume for her. I did find another tiger costume I could put her in, and she loved it. In fact, I ran the Turkey Trot when she was two or maybe three in my tiger costume, with her in her tiger costume in the running stroller, and her wielding a tiger puppet, creating a kind of super-meta tiger situation that I hope some people noticed. That was the most fun iteration of the Trot to date. She had a blast being pushed in the costume in the stroller by a tiger, with everyone cheering us on. It's a European-style 5k, and I'm not sure what that means except that in the two loops you run on the course, you have to jump over a hay bale and then immediately over a mud pit, which I guess reminds one of Europe? This is the spot where most of the crowd congregates, wanting to watch people jump it or run through it. In the previous year the race had a little area you could go through to bail out if you didn't want to jump or run through the mud, which was kind of against the spirit of the thing, but the year I ran it with my daughter in the running stroller they had removed that option, a fact I only realized when we got right up to it and there was no option except to go over the hay bale and through the muddy water pit. Athena was shrieking with glee, which was good because it was either that or she'd flip out with fear or anger. I popped a wheelie to bump awkwardly over the hay bale. Going through the water, unfortunately I lost the back wheel on the running stroller and I could hear the collective gasp from the crowd watching us. I slapped it back in, to cheers and laughter, and on the second time through people were screaming TIGER, TIGER! as we went over and through again, and finished hard.

It was an exhilarating experience, even if we were not fast and I nearly barfed from the heat and exertion.

I mean to tell you that I have come to love wearing costumes, even if I only wear them on occasion. So when I put my Predator mask on I feel differently, but I also *move* differently in it: slowly, by necessity, and with deliberation.

I know mine is a crappy copy. I give it no name. I make no post. I claim no authenticity. "Making a suit has been a life long dream," says MystxXxHunter, and they're getting closer to achieving it. "I'm a naturally good artist," they write, "[but] this is no easy feat. . . . I have a left hand glove. Custom. Took 40hrs to sculpt." They report the head so far has taken between 300 and 500 hours, and they had to go back and start from scratch: "Nothing says fun like resculpting half a predhead. . . . I wish I would have read this [site] sooner and had it branded into my brain the seriousness of what I'm getting into."

TKZOMBIE responds, "I have my Predator now and it's been a love/hate relationship. She's a beautiful creation but had I known how much maintenance is required and that it can't be put on by yourself I'd have never gone forward with it." It takes (at least) two to make a thing go right, so even though the predator hunts alone, a predator's not a predator without its prey. Wreav, who wrote the 2017 Predator Costume Manual Guide, says: "My first suit required two people to help me put on." Some collaboration will be required, which, it seems, is half the pleasure.

WE'RE ALMOST HALFWAY through the film, and I'm having doubts about the metaphor I've chosen to filter the filter through—or did it choose me for its grueling, its cooling mist? Like a pederast, did it groom me from the start, understanding my vulnerability to bodysuits and a chiseling, quivering manfulness and action punctuated by conversation meant to say something definitive about what it is or was to be or be alive in 1987, which was being kicked in the face and brain and balls simultaneously?

Which was: it hurt to be alive and be embodied; which was it hurt to be pressed like that, to bind our breasts like that, to lie flat like that, like flowers in the pages of a book that was the '80s even though we didn't know it then I mean we didn't know what it meant to be the '80s then, what the '80s meant to men I mean would come to mean to men or how it drooled its shine on men and interceded with history on our behalf.

Or is it a sieve I mean and not a filter? Is it Billy Idol I mean and not another singer? He is still in time: at first glance he looks the same: spiked hair, smooth face, that smirk. Is it a Ho Ho I was eating or a Zinger or a cheaper copy stolen from the Citgo where we tried to steal the store on Thursday afternoons? (On its shelves we found our woe and kept on eating it as if to prove by our consumption we were presently alive.)

Memory: is it a screen on which I'm watching Idol mean and become a feature of the culture? Somehow he has come to matter. He doesn't mean anything more to me than Predator: they're both lip-curl and spectacle and lack of girls and the statistical mean of every man I knew or believed in 1987 that I could one day be, the year we tried for the fourth time unsuccessfully to blow up that Citgo and the only Lamborghini I ever saw in person. I mean, you see a Lambo after watching *Rambo: First Blood Part Two*, and it's a guard tower you want to wire to blow, like punishing success, and know a bottle rocket is one way to harness fire when you're from where I am from. We don't have that many ideas, but in this way we learn to move the world. A pet's flinch, the finch's pissed zigzag to avoid the arc and the report: these are the signs we are capable of making. So what if we know no one is impressed by our loneliness? Failing this, what did we graduate to next?

I misread the welcome sign at the state's edge and think it says, *Michigan: Bigger Restrooms, Fatter Dancers*. It's since been shot a couple of times. Someone replaces it. Someone takes a gun to it again. Repeat. This goes on for longer than you'd expect.

ANNA, OUR SOLE FEMALE CHARACTER, occupies the center of the movie, fifty-three minutes and seventeen seconds in. I pause at the exact midpoint, and the shot is of her hands, folded, zip-tied. Still covered in streaks of Hawkins's blood, she contemplates the creature's glowing green blood smeared on her pants. She almost strokes the blood. Here she's sexier than we see her elsewhere, streaked in sweat and mud. These shots of her (again, I want to point out, our sole female character) are odd. What is her role here after all? Is she here to contrast the ways of the men in the film? She's not a love interest, and she's not exactly someone to protect. She is an asset for Dillon, as he explained, and Dutch does protect her, in his way, but unlike in *Commando*, where there are two female characters (Schwarzenegger's character's daughter, played by Alyssa Milano, and a woman he kind of kidnaps who ends up helping him, played by Rae Dawn Chong), Anna's here for unknown reasons. Is the thought from the studio that you needed at least one female character, you know, for the ladies to identify with? Or to make it a little less of a festival of men? She does offer contrast to their sheer boyness, and also she's not one of them. She's not American and is the only one of them who's not explicitly military (though I guess she was with the guerrillas, whatever that means in *Predator*). She starts out as an enemy but is about to become an ally when they realize what they are up against.

So far Anna's only spoken Spanish, to Dillon and Poncho, which isn't translated in the film. McTiernan tells us this: "I seem to always get caught in these scenes with characters speaking a foreign language back and forth. I think where it came from was [as a kid] spending so much time watching foreign movies, and I would never read the subtitles. I really didn't care what people said. I still don't. I get into all kinds of trouble because I still don't care what people say on-screen. I care what they look like when they say it, and how it sounds. It's part of this notion I've got that movies are really music. They're not photographed plays: they're a completely separate idea. They're much closer to music than the theater. . . .

The audience hears *how* they say something instead of what they say." This is true. We don't care a great deal for what many of these characters say; we want to watch their mouths and their bodies move. We want to listen to "Long Tall Sally" on repeat.

What did Carrillo make of her experience working on the film? She says in a 2014 interview, "The only thing I learned from making *Predator* was to be able to survive among a bunch of horny, macho, stupid, muscle men. I am very proud of that."

We see all of that—the macho, the stupid, the muscle, and the horny—in these shots. The camera lingers on her in this scene in the way it does more often on the men in the film: hornily. She too is now greased up and glistening in the dusky light of the jungle. Anna's something for us to look at here. Maybe she's a way for us to sublimate some of these urges we're feeling, watching the movie, and point them in a different direction?

Perhaps. But she's also a witness to their violence, and another kind of answer. We'll see later that the Predator will not attack her since she is unarmed, so she's also here to make that point.

CUT BACK TO A SHOT of the creature, injured, sitting on a log, as it deactivates its camouflage cloak and attends to its wound—a wound only it and Anna know about. The camera fetishizes the thing's alien tools, reminiscent in their way of the homemade gynecological tools devised by the twins in David Cronenberg's *Dead Ringers*, a film I saw in the theater in 1988 and that, at thirteen, I had absolutely no idea what to do with. I still feel seared by the experience. I value this impression so much I haven't watched it since, though I bought it on DVD many years ago. I wonder if another viewing will somehow erase the effect it had on me, or if it will bring it back the way watching *Predator* at forty-five does. This is a silly scene really. I guess it shows the alien is vulnerable, so there is that. It roars in pain. It is no longer unscarred by this hunt. Perhaps we're meant to understand that now it's personal.

If you look at revision 6 of the script, dated January 30, 1987, in which the film was still at this point titled "Hunter," you can see how the story evolved. At this point the script shows a scene in the alien's "oval CHAMBER made of an otherworldly looking metal with a strange copperlike patina, its interior bathed in INTENSE BLUE LIGHT. In the chamber is Hawkins' SKULL CAP and SPINAL COLUMN still attached." The whole script does the ALL-CAPS EMPHASIS at what may or may not be random times, and it accentuates the somewhat unhinged experience of reading and reinforces the feeling that the writers—John and Jim Thomas—are SUPER INTO the coolness of every EPIC effect in every scene. Like, why wouldn't you capitalize OTHERWORLDLY or METAL or COPPERLIKE or PATINA? These individual capitalizations are a function of "each writer's unique style," according to "6 Things to Capitalize in Your Screenplay," which advises, "Not every sound, visual effect, and prop needs to be capitalized. The number one priority is that your script is as easy to read as possible. . . . Keep your use of capitalization for this scenario to a minimum." This is not advice the Thomas brothers took. This scene does not appear in the movie, perhaps because it would have been expensive to film (and perhaps also unnecessary). *Predator* was filmed, of course, before the age of omnipresent CGI.

Aficionados of the movie know that, in the earlier stages of moviemaking, a then-unknown Belgian actor named Jean-Claude Van Damme was cast as the Predator. There's footage of him in a pretty-stupid-looking red dinosaur suit that you can find online, and it's bizarre to watch, having seen the finished film, which casts a compelling spell with its vastly better practical monster effects and suit. According to oral histories, Van Damme left for one or more of several reasons: he hated the look of it (which is correct: it's stupid as hell), it was unimaginably cumbersome and hot to wear, and he couldn't do stunts or fight in it (Van Damme would become known for his epic martial arts abilities and would go on to become an action star). So he left the film and they instead hired Kevin Peter Hall, who was at least a foot taller than Van Damme. He would go on to play the monster Harry in *Harry and the Hendersons*.

Blood—in the script: BLOOD—is everywhere in this and most other action movies of the era. It's sprayed across Anna's face as Hawkins is eviscerated in front of her. It drips down the leaves from the bodies hoisted into the trees. It's smeared across her chest in the aftermath. Blain had no time to bleed, he informed us, until he did. And the blood also echoes through the AIDS epidemic at the time. Blood, then, was an agent of infection.

Blood is strange, isn't it? It's that thing that animates us, and it's what we lose when cut or separated. It's what connects us to our biological families, we say. It's what makes brothers—like screenwriters John and Jim Thomas, or like my brother and me—mean more to each other than anyone else can. There's that weird trope of "blood brothers"—where does it come from?—that we remember from childhood, in which two of us would cut our hands and touch those cuts together, exchanging, so we imagined, blood. HIV and AIDS changed our relationship with blood in ways that are still abstract to me, as someone who never particularly had to worry about contracting it. Still, you never know. I'd had unprotected sex. I'd exchanged bodily fluids with others. It wasn't impossible. I was aware of AIDS as a possibility—one of the many dangers of sex you didn't have to worry about with pornography.

Action and horror movies fetishize blood. It's a grand visual, a signifier of something bad having happened, so much of us having now come out of us. It's also among the very easiest of special effects: what looks like blood never is.

Unlike the unfilmed scene from the script set inside the alien's ship, the next scene from the script was actually filmed, and is one of my very favorite moments in the movie. Mac's soliloquy at the fifty-seven-minute mark is a tender moment addressed to his dead friend Blain. It goes on for almost forty seconds, ending with "I'm gonna cut your name into him."

Nothing Tender

Nothing tender would still run free by morning.
—PAUL MONETTE, *PREDATOR*

SURVIVOR GUILT 2: It's the sequel to *Survivor Guilt*, in which those of us who made it through the first film cry and stare at each other with surprise in our eyes, and see if we respond. We do some stuff. We write it down. Because guilt is hard to film we screw or blow stuff up. We disrobe because it's sexier when we do it with our bodies. Some of us are gone and some are left. There seems to be no reason why.

In film the reason why is obvious: the biggest star is the one who makes it through. We remember 1996's *Executive Decision*, in which Steven Seagal, the seeming star, gets killed about thirty minutes in, and from there our expectations are set adrift: if the action star dies, what the fuck are we supposed to do after that? It's a good trick, and from what we know about the ego of Steven Seagal, that couldn't have been an easy sell. This movie was written by John and Jim Thomas, who also wrote *Predator*. The rest of the movie goes on without Seagal, but all I remember is how surprised I was to see him (seem to) die. How rare the exception that proves the rule! After that, I understood that anything could happen (though I don't remember what did).

Monette feels it too. When those around you die and die and die, you might wonder why it's you who's still alive. It's mostly chance, or hesitance, you'd think. Is my being alive simply because I lived or loved less? Is it random? (Probably.) A line from one of Monette's journals after Rog's death, seemingly disconnected from anything else on the page: "What am I doing here?"

Dear Dutch, have you ever thought to ask what you are *doing* in *Predator*?

Dear Dutch, what do you feel in *Predator*?

Do you feel in *Predator*?

You feel betrayed by your government (all of us will be betrayed if we wait long enough, I know) and by Dillon, your erstwhile friend. Now several on your team are dead. That's on you, you know. You feel hunted. Some fear, surely. Wonder, confronting the alien: the world you believed you were in has now expanded.

We don't have time to bleed. We don't have time to feel. The typical logic of the action film is that there is no time to feel, much less to mourn or to ruminate. All feeling is delayed. Without seeing our protagonists feeling, *we* are the place where all the feelings accrue. So when the bad guy/thing is finally killed we feel lighter by default, because we have to in order to survive. It's effective. If we were to feel—to really feel—for these characters, their deaths would be as unbearable as the deaths of those we love, which we want to feel as rarely as possible.

In *Predator*, however, this isn't strictly true. There is love between these men, particularly Blain and Mac. There's time given to feeling, even a little grieving, at least after the shooting is over. Here's Mac's whole minute-long soliloquy (which is an actual, technical soliloquy; I'm not using the term for emphasis):

Here we are again bro, just you and me, same kind of moon, same kind of jungle. . . . Remember: whole platoon, thirty-two men, chopped into meat. We walk out, just you and me, nobody else. Right on top, huh? Not a scratch . . . Not a fuckin' scratch. You know who ever got you. They'll come back again. And when he does I'm gonna cut your name right into him . . . I'm gonna cut your name into him.

In *Terminator 2*, Arnold's most famous line is "I'll be back." I heard it (hearted it) again in Monette's *Borrowed Time*:

He'd come back; they swore it. I sat at the desk unable to sleep, working numbly on *Predator* for an hour or so. I called UCLA at two and again at three. They said they were having trouble keeping his fever under control, but otherwise he was stable. You force yourself not to think about the pain, where it hurt this time and how bad. . . . I went to bed certain he'd be responding to the drug within a few hours. I would not see the dying.

In *Predator* we see the dying of the men but not of the alien. Where does all that feeling go?

ALL THAT FEELING does have to get channeled somewhere, so in this instance part of it ends up directed toward a boar that accidentally enters the camp, sets off the trip wires, and gets stabbed to death by a frenzied and grief-stricken Mac. After he's killed the boar, having spent some of that tenderness, the guys come upon him mumbling to himself as he rolls off of it, covered in blood: "Got you, motherfucker."

Then what he's killed is revealed. Poncho asks, "Do you think you could've found something bigger?" Unlike the other jokes in this movie, this is a good joke because it is a cruel one, and if you're like me, you know it hurts, and it's funny because it does, and the only response to this is the one in the film: fuck you. Neither the joke nor the line is in the script. It eases things to have it there.

Here's another bit in the script that doesn't make it into the film: a scene in which a chameleon crawls onto Anna's arm then back onto the leaf and she watches it change color. It feels too on the nose to me so seems a good cut, or perhaps they couldn't get the lizard to do what it was supposed to do and gave it up.

An hour into the movie someone finally asks Anna her name. It turns out that she speaks English.

Here she also finally tells them that they must have wounded the alien. She saw its blood.

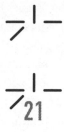

If It Bleeds, We Can Kill It

AS I'M WORKING ON THIS CHAPTER I see news not only of one but of two horrific mass shootings in America: outside Atlanta, Georgia (eight dead), and in Boulder, Colorado (ten dead). What a shocker: both shooters are men. Both shooters were twenty-one. That doesn't include the other 105 mass shootings in the United States as of March 23, 2021. Already this year, 122 people have been killed; 378 have been wounded. At least no shootings so far have occurred at a school or university, and none at places of worship. But the year is young. I find myself scrolling through the list of dead—awfully—looking for highlights I can pull to prove my point, but the point is that there were 105 mass shootings I hadn't even heard of, that hadn't hit the headlines in Tucson. Three of them occurred in Phoenix, Arizona. A couple in Michigan, though not particularly close to where I've lived. Another one in the small town where I went to college: Galesburg, Illinois. Those data points stand out to me by proximity to where I've lived, so they feel a little more alive to me. Otherwise it all feels like data, which it both is and is not. These numbers also represent a whole lot of *people*.

After Sandy Hook I thought surely *this* must be the point at

which *something* had to change. After the Orlando nightclub shooting, I thought the same. After Vegas. I thought this after Tucson.
And little of any consequence has changed. How many communities need to be hit before we can call gun violence what it very
obviously is: an epidemic? How many kids need to get shot before we actually, finally take some action? If you've followed these
stories—and how could you not over the past decade, or follow
that even further back—then you know how intractable this problem is. How big it seems. How invulnerable. And how stupid.

DUTCH RESPONDS, "If it bleeds, we can kill it."

I feel this way about the wildly out-of-control strain of internet so-called masculinity I've been talking about here. If it bleeds,
we can kill it, even if I'm not sure how. Step one is seeing the thing
clearly, even if it means using an alien's eyes to see what else it is
we're seeing when we watch this movie over and over.

In the movie it's an opportunity, a note of hope. When we
know the creature can be wounded, maybe we can finally feel like
we can do something about it. So it's time again for action. Here's
a montage of the team getting ready to trap and kill the thing,
or try to anyhow. Here's them chopping vines. Here's them pulling trees. Here's them carrying rope they made from vines. Here's
them setting traps. Here's them wrapping vines around wooden
pegs. Here's them building things.

I love montages. They're like skipping ahead in flashes: we don't
need to see everything. A few details will do. And these flashes
pit man against nature. Man against man for a moment, as Dillon
says, "You really think this Boy Scout bullshit is gonna work?" And
as Dutch responds, "Instead of complaining, maybe you should
help." Dillon acknowledges the point, so help he does. Here's
Dillon helping. Here's Billy bending a tree. Here we see Dutch and
a shirtless Dillon and Poncho pulling on a rope, apparently bending a big tree to the ground. The camera loves the men, especially
with their shirts off, working all in tandem now. In the next shot,

we see Billy joins them. It all looks pretty elaborate. This is the kind of thing I thought I would be doing at Boy Scout camp as a kid, not whittling sticks and eating cattail roots.

From the script, though not in the film: "Morning passes. Fog lifts as the sun creeps into the jungle. Insects swarm and are fed upon by BIRDS and other predators." Again a good cut. First, we don't really think of most BIRDS as predators (though of course they are, as are we), and second, it would be a bit hard to film; and third, we get it, man. Mostly this film skips the obvious visual metaphors. This I appreciate and you should too.

There is, however, a great moment in 1990's inferior but certainly watchable *Predator 2* in which for some reason the lead, Danny Glover, stares into a shop window's display of taxidermied animals: a bear, a baboon, a hawk, and a bunch of deer and birds—not that far off from the scenes in the International Wildlife Museum, if less well lit. He sees himself in the glass and pauses: Is he predator or prey? Collector or collected? Whether he makes anything of that contemplation, we don't know.

I forgot the subway scene from *Predator 2*, in which we watch a group of pierced and tattooed punks harassing people in an LA subway car. They settle on a bespectacled, milquetoast-looking businessman and pull a knife on him. Then he somewhat tremulously pulls a gun on them. Then one of the punks pulls a much bigger gun on *him*. Then five separate bystanders on the subway car pull guns on *them*. *Then* two detectives pull guns on the punks and try to talk down all the passengers: "We don't need any rush hour Rambos." Then, of course, the Predator arrives and pulls rank, and the whole thing goes off the rails. In this future, everyone's armed, so everyone's a predator, so everyone can count as prey.

BACK TO OUR PREVIOUSLY scheduled programming, and we enter another moment of silence in *Predator*, in which the team, having built their traps, now waits for something to happen. I'm reminded of the loud-quiet-loud dynamic of late '80s alternative music best embodied by the Pixies and those who picked up the grunge torch and ran with it lit, and how my friends in the military describe much of their experience as "hurry up and wait." In this movie, as in many action movies, we alternate between frenzy and silence, each reinforcing and giving a sense of scale and definition to the other.

Speaking of scale, here comes the epic simile, one of my favorite moves in Monette's *Predator*:

> Their dozen wars suddenly amounted to nothing, and their massive kills and their awesome bravery and luck were as meaningless as the random swarms of bees that floated like liquid gunfire in the deep of the woods.

I mean, give a poet a squad of guys with guns and you're going to get a bone bouquet, a gone bouquet eventually, so I don't think it's too much to compare *Predator* to *The Iliad*: in the novelization Monette's already doing it for you. Here we zoom out and then back in on guns and blood. War backdrops both and allows for meaning in beauty amid the terror of it, the bore and buzz of it. Between killings we watch our men interact and talk: it may be only here that they are able to communicate this way. Mac and Blain provide the best evidence of tenderness, but the spark between all the men arcs and makes the movie go.

Both stories are tragedies: most of the people we care about in *Predator* die and one by one their stories are subsumed into the vessel that is Dutch, who erases himself as he covers himself in mud in order to finally kill the thing. In victory, he will look scarred and should be: almost all of those he cared for died. Only a stranger will make it out with him. As Monette worked on the novelization many of those he cared for were lost amid the tragedy of HIV. They, too, died one by one in a war our government refused to recognize.

So Monette knew something about how the face of death presents itself. Sometimes all we have is moments, one still shot after another, before they're gone. Sometimes all there is to do is write them down.

Most of us don't experience *Predator* as a tragedy. But if you keeping going on past the end of a tragedy sometimes it turns into something else, I want to tell my depressive self at seventeen. I want to tell that to myself at seven, after my mother died and what I did then was channel all my energy into playing video games and blowing things up and trying to leave a scar on the world.

If you channel enough energy into a franchise or a mythology you begin to think you own it. You begin to think it loves you back. Luckily for me, when I lost myself in games it was *Space Invaders* and *Yars' Revenge*, relatively rudimentary games that won't take all you can put into them and transform you through your attention to their every nuance and mechanic. If I'd had *Fallout 3* or *Mass Effect* at that age, I don't know if I would have ever got myself back out again.

What we want to call tragedy all has to do with scope and time and POV where you start and stop paying attention to the plot. You could follow Dutch another fifty years and watch him die of mouth or lung cancer (all those cigars could finally bring him low, even if nothing else could) alone in a hospital bed, still trying to tell us about the alien and what it brought out of him back then in that jungle. If we follow Schwarzenegger long enough we will eventually be reminded of his flawed humanity.

I'm reminded that how good we feel about the things we see is dependent on our closeness to the action. We all know our Woody Allen (comedy = tragedy + time), though it's gotten harder to cite Woody Allen without having to also have to talk about Woody Allen, which I don't quite know enough about to really want to do except to note that here's another example of a dude whom I can no longer think about without feeling rage. It's not that I feel the disconnect between cause and effect, the firing of the guns and the killing of the men in the movie (though I do). Neither of these things seemed real then, and they still don't now, one way in which the film is tolerable. For most of us guns aren't quite real until someone in our lives gets shot. Bombs aren't real until your friend blows off their hand. Guns are merely props on the wall until they're not. And obviously we're not concerned with the fate of the guards in the camp eating lunch when they get blown up. Is that not a tragedy? Did they not have families?

We don't see, so we must suppose they all died trying to kill our guys, which surely can't totally be true. You'd think most of them would have run away, facing a clearly superior enemy, and taken their chances in the jungle. I mean, fuck it, how much were they paid, if they were paid at all? At least a few must've seen the writing on the wall and been shot in the back as they fled into the jungle. In the novelization they're hunted down and killed, one by one, but I imagine the memoir of the "guerrilla" who escaped the Americans' assault. And even if the guys trying in the helicopter got shot and blown up when they were only trying to escape, there's the mission to think of here: what were our guys supposed to do? Just *let* the thing take off?

And what is the Predator supposed to *do* after watching all of this? *Not* go after these action star behemoths, the kind who took out a whole camp of enemies, all bent on killing them? If the Predator didn't believe it had found a worthy foe before, it sure does now, having seen what we just saw.

And what are *we* supposed to do? *Not* root for our protagonists as they are picked off, one by one, by a technologically superior life-form, leaving Dutch the Emptiest as our sole vessel, the one who fights for what we as humans are supposed to represent, or whatever?

I mean, we are machines, made to feel and fall and so we feel and fall. I mean, sometimes you have to play your role. That's what the *Iliad* teaches us. That's what action films teach us once we get to know their grammar.

If you watch a bunch you come to take pleasure in their similarity. They're like romance novels. They're like porn. You know what it is you want, but you want it with a variation every time. The Predators say so too. When Dutch kills one, another arrives in *Predator 2*, and more, eventually, in the other sequels. Killing each one only makes us more appealing targets for the next time around. I mean, how we get to feel about our story depends when you stop paying attention.

And if that's the case, what is actually gained by all this Schwarzeneggerian struggle? A few more years of warming earth and hotter weather, bringing even more hard-core Predators? What was gained by fighting a pandemic for another couple of years before succumbing to it? What are a few more years worth? What is another hour of the movie worth? And what is gained by engaging our passions for anything really? Are we any different from ants struggling mightily to wrestle some overlarge piece of food back to their colony and—failing or succeeding, what's the difference there? I mean to ask: Where do we find the meaning in our evenings / our readings? Maybe it's only in giving ourselves over to something that we find ourselves at all.

Since the films frequently and increasingly mention that the creatures come in the hottest years, and set the whole enterprise against our own overpopulating, superheating exploitation of the earth, why do we believe we should get to survive anyway? On account of our thoughtful stewardship of the planet? Maybe the world would be better if the aliens picked off the most hardcore among us, the ones who've proved that they can do maximum damage to the rest of us? Perhaps through predation and natural selection we'd soon enough be gentler humans, easier on the planet?

I'd love to see a *Predator* sequel set in the American life of mass shootings we find ourselves living in 2021.

I mean, maybe we're better with a threat. Maybe all we need is a shooter in our church or in our school, or a shoulder-mounted laser cannon pointed at us by an invisible alien to get us to finally freaking be our better selves, like the Misfit said? We have better selves. I'm pretty sure we have some better selves. Maybe there's only one way to find out.

From the novelization:

This whole scene seemed all wrong. The violence was crude and stupid, and the enemy was dumb. . . . "Predator," Billy stated flatly, his face showing no emotion.

22

Only in the Hottest Years

AT 1:04, we look at Mac again in the silence, waiting, shaving sweat off his blank face with a disposable razor. The third time he does it we watch the blade pause and press in against his cheek. That blankness is covering terror up. Or at least tension. The plastic snaps under the pressure and we see the blood bead out. I presume—but am not sure—this is a special effect. If so, it's a little one and an effective one. We know what that pain feels like in a way we hopefully will never know what it's like to be shot by an alien's shoulder cannon.

LET'S BE HONEST: like all films 2-adorned, *Predator 2* is way worse than the first. You're immediately thinking of counterexamples: *Evil Dead 2*, maybe. *Empire Strikes Back* doesn't count: a change in title keeps it from being *Star Wars 2*, and as the nerds will tell you it's actually Episode V, roman numeral and all, a fact I feel obliged to keep explaining to my daughter as we watch the movies in the order of their release. I can feel you if we want to talk video games (*Star Control 2*, for instance; *Mass Effect 2* or *Borderlands 2*;

actually a lot of 2 games are good because gameplay is much easier to repeat, improve, and perfect than narrative).

The film's 1997 looks like junk: messy, hot, clichéd "urban jungle" to update the actual jungle of the first film. It's set in Los Angeles, a city in the middle of a heat wave and a gang war between the Colombian and Jamaican drug cartels that the cops are engaged in when the camera moves past the establishing shot, a joke beginning in foliage and giving way to city skyline. It's the way you might imagine a future LA in 1990, chaotic and combustible, if not quite the exact mix that would produce the LA riots. Cops here are at best ineffectual and overwhelmed. At every turn we're reminded that it's hot, hot, hot. The predatory media are everywhere, drawn by and contributing to the blood, violence, and viscera. Bullets fly. Shutters click. The mercury only rises.

Both *Predator 2* and *Predator* get this right: the world is getting hotter. I know: I live in Arizona. If the aliens only come in the hottest years, we should look forward to more of them descending on our planet as we heat it. As of 2020, each of the last three years has been historically the hottest, each kicking the last one's ass. And you could see that trend in the late '80s too. In a 1989 interview about the film, *Predator 2* costar Gary Busey prognosticates: "What if it's 110 degrees all over the world in 1997? We could be headed that way. Who knows?" Well, now we know: the trend looks more gradual than that but difficult to stop. It hit 115 last week where I live. It'll be 116 today.

Predator 2's slowness is worse, less managed than the first. Or do I think that because I was older when I first saw it? Because I prefer the '80s action idiom to the '90s? Because the first is remote and wild and what I am accustomed to—where I'm from, my Michigan—is remote and wild?

This is the version of LA that drew Ice Cube to sample *Predator 2* in his 1992 album *The Predator*, which is, like *Predator 2*, a mix of violence, guns, juvenile jokes that haven't aged superwell, justifiable and entertaining outrage at police violence that feels very much of the moment, writing this in 2021, and some timeless bits.

On and in *Predator 2* and *The Predator*, shots ring out cartoonishly. Like the Predator, Cube represents himself as top dog: it's always he who kills (not he who's killed) and always he who fucks (not he who's fucked). This is how he matters: his swagger and his potency, his samples and his flow, his talk of guns, his anger at the cops and a whitened world that has still not come to terms with itself a couple of decades later.

He is not cloaked (unless being Black in a white world is a kind of cloak, which it is, and it's a reverse cloak too), and that year both he and LA had the world's attention.

Twenty-five years on, when the rest of 1992's cultural contributions have mostly washed away (consider some of the other number 1 albums released that year: Billy Ray Cyrus's *Some Gave All*, Kris Kross's *Totally Krossed Out*, Def Leppard's *Adrenalize*, a couple of Garth Brooks albums, and Michael Bolton's *Timeless: The Classics*), we got left with Cube, timeless as we keep making him. Of the year's top ten films, *Aladdin* sticks around (2019 brought it back again), but *Home Alone 2* continues to tell us nothing about the world, nor does *Basic Instinct* probably. But let that go, Abednego, and we're left with *Predator*, skeletal and pissed and resonant and always hunting something somewhere.

The movie still nails its moments of sharp critique: a kid with a toy Uzi invents enemies in a cemetery and sprays them with imaginary bullets. It's a prescient scene: unlike some cops, the Predator sizes up the kid and deems him not a threat or legit target, though at first glance the gun looks real enough. In this way we see the civilized in the Predator and wonder what became of the civilized in us.

Who knows why it doesn't kill the boy: his size, perhaps, or his obvious glee as he pretends to shoot his pretend guns into the world. Maybe it recognizes a familiar approach to the world. Or might the way we regard our young be less gentle than the creature's? Or it might have something to do with fear. Predator fears nothing, we come to learn, but all we do is fear, particularly those unlike us.

That kid might as well have been me. I shot the world or shot at it at least, even if I never saw it bleed, or not because of me or anything I did. It seemed most days it had no time for me or for my attempts at incisions. If we didn't have toy guns we'd make swords and whip each other with them. We made our bombs. Smashed what we could. Chucked rocks at cars. Killed little animals to prove something to ourselves. One friend with his homemade guillotine. The best gun toys were the least like toys, the right size, the sort that might inflame a Predator, without the mandated orange ends to signify our play. This was the age of jarts, metal lawn darts you'd throw in the air, descendants of plumbata, Roman war darts that were meant to pierce the skull. We'd throw them in the air and close our eyes and wait to see what happened. No one caught one in the head. We made homemade bazookas, too, that were pretty cool. And what a word: *bazooka*. Can't think of one more fun, can you?

I don't only mean the barely edible gum Bazooka that came wrapped in a waxed paper comic, but the portable rocket launcher used to blow up tanks: its magic is in how it wraps up both senses. Bob "Bazooka" Burns invented the bazooka, a wind instrument that sounds like a joke, as a joke. A few years later a general noted the new weapon's likeness to the musical instrument, and the name caught on, possibly also as a joke. After World War II, Topps debuted the gum, pink, wrapped in a red and white and blue comic. It's a gum so dense you can't blow bubbles with it, or I couldn't anyway. I'd buy the comics forty years later from the little store at the end of Bremer Road and try to chew the desiccated stuff before spitting it out into the ditch and trying to read the comic it was wrapped in, because kids liked comics and so, I thought, should I. Eating it was a little bit like being shot, I thought, or blown up; maybe that was simply a story I told myself. I suppose they were going for "an explosion of flavor" or perhaps it's the mouthfeel of the word they liked and its exuberance sense of linguistic play or maybe it was the violence chewed up in the name, which did, I should admit, keep me buying it for quite a few years.

Oh, hey, *Terminator 2*; *Spider-Man 2*; *Toy Story 2*; *The Godfather: Part II*; *Star Trek II*; *Friday the 13th Part 2*.

THIS IS THE DREAM of science fiction: as a bunch of fucked-up humans on this planet we are divided by race, sex, class, the differences we perceive between ourselves, but when threatened real bad we can finally come together. Of the group, only Dutch and Hawkins and Blain were white, and now there's only Dutch alive. Dillon, who has been shown to be a somewhat bad actor and a villain, is now on the team. Dutch even cuts Anna loose, saying, "This thing is hunting us. All of us. You know that. We need everyone." When confronted by the extraterrestrial, suddenly we are literally all in this thing together. When confronted by tragedy we are brought together—for a while at least. It's hard here not to think of the shooting of my congresswoman, Gabrielle Giffords, and the sudden sense of belonging I felt with my adopted home-town of Tucson. I had not felt that way before. Tucson has a lot of crazies I don't identify with much of the time. But when confronted with an incident as shocking as this, I suddenly felt part of that *we* for the first time. And that was on account of a human man (if a fucked-up one) with a gun. I, too, have been a human man with a gun. I grew up a human man with a gun among other human men with guns. Now I live among many more human men with guns (and plenty of human women with guns). My brother still has guns, but I don't anymore. Haven't for years. I feel further from my brother—politically, religiously—than I ever have before. But give us *Predator* and we're who we used to be. It's *Predator* that brings us together. Is it *Predator* that keeps us together? And way more of us have guns now than when I grew up anyway, and I feel less and less comfortable with that every day. Imagine what might happen to our shared sense of *we* if a camouflaging alien showed up in our driveway or our Safeway.

I WATCHED 1984's *Red Dawn* last night with some friends. We've been watching mostly bad '70s and '80s movies Wednesday nights together amidst the pandemic. All of us had seen it as kids, and I'd rewatched it at least a couple of times that decade and at least once as an adult. If you're not familiar, it's a fantasy in which Russia, Nicaragua, and Cuba suddenly invade America—particularly a small town in Colorado: someplace remote and survivalist. A bunch of teenagers take to the woods and mount an armed insurgent resistance against the invading forces, largely successfully. It's a prepper's dream, in which guns don't kill people, people kill people, and hard and seemingly unreasonable American fathers turn out to have prepared their kids well for life opposing a dictatorship. It's a well-made movie, actually; it's well acted (it features a bunch of young actors who would become much more famous for other roles: Charlie Sheen, Patrick Swayze, Lea Thompson, and Jennifer Grey, to name a few), has a huge budget (they have actual tanks and planes), and is relatively well written and well directed. It gets worse as it goes, though, escalating quickly as the kids move from harassing a few Russians to taking on tanks and blowing up planes with an unusual number of RPGs, which are technically bazookas. The movie stands up, though it stands up stronger as propaganda: how effectively and obviously it created the fantasy that lives on to this day in Upper Michigan and Arizona, and a lot of the rest of the country, that stockpiling RPGs is the only response to tyranny.

No doubt: it is violent. According to the *New York Times*, "The National Coalition on Television Violence has condemned the summer hit 'Red Dawn' as the most violent movie ever made. The fantasy about third-world troops invading a small Colorado town averages 134 acts of violence an hour." It also noted that the movies released in the summer of 1984 were the most violent ever in the history of the industry, "averaging 28.5 violent acts an hour," which *Red Dawn* exceeded by nearly 400 percent.

At the time it was released, the *Guinness Book of World Records* considered it the most violent film ever made.

In 2009 the *National Review* included it on the list of the Best Conservative Movies of the past twenty-five years. It was also the first film to be rated PG-13.

According to director John Milius, "That movie's not about the Russians; it's about the federal government." Very well then.

PREDATOR DIRECTOR John McTiernan talks about *Predator*'s gun violence in the director's commentary for the fifteenth anniversary collector's edition DVD, reproduced in the more recent Blu-ray releases:

> When I first went to work on this project, I had the feeling that people had a sort of perverse fascination with pictures of guns firing, literally an almost pornographic desire. And I said to myself, okay if you want pictures of guns firing, I'll give you pictures of guns firing, so I created this sequence where they take all of their guns and they blaze away continually for five minutes flat, and they flatten the jungle and they mow down *every*thing. And what I was really doing was sort of, in the Australian phrase, taking the piss out of [war too], to quietly ridicule the desire to see pictures of guns firing.
>
> All of this is the moral separate piece where I said in no circumstance were there to be human beings in front of the guns firing. In fact, the point of all the firing was, as the man says as soon as they stop shooting, *we hit nothing*. The whole point is the impotence of all the guns, which is exactly the opposite of what I believed I was being hired to sell.
>
> Studios really are a bit disingenuous. This movie and some of the ones that followed it really did carry a pornographic desire to market images of guns firing. It was in corporate purpose,

and this was, I wanted the job, so this was my compromise for that. I gave them all the gunfire they could possibly desire and at the same time I didn't really advertise to little kids how wonderful guns are. Or at least I thought I wasn't.

Now I did the same thing in the next movie: I created a scene in *Die Hard* where they BLAZE away and we get five minutes of guns firing and they're shooting *glass*. The point was they're not shooting at *people*. Now some of the people involved in this movie have since put that same sequence in just about every movie they make and are involved in—with several differences. They forget to take the people out in front of the guns. So you get a sequence where they blaze away for five minutes and kill people or images of people, and then completely act utterly innocent and puzzled when something like Columbine happens.

Hearing McTiernan tell me this on my 146th viewing of the movie validated a lot of the way I understand the movie's various layers and agendas. I love the movie for its base genre elements— explosions, one-liners, huge and ripped dudes, fantastic violence, blood, badassery—as much as anyone does, but it gradually became obvious to me that *Predator*, though an action movie, clearly means to satirize action movies. As McTiernan explains, much of the first third of the movie was shot by the second unit, most obviously the giant action sequence of the team decimating the guerrilla compound. He's not superhappy, clearly, with the work of the second unit. He's got some shit to say about the static nature of the camerawork. While that whole sequence does kick ass, and kicking ass is important, it also feels a little bit obligatory. It's the closest this movie comes to those other movies—*Commando*, *Rambo*, etc.—and so it's also where it's least itself. If you've seen those movies you've seen that sequence before: not in its specifics, but in its grammar and its mechanics. The steps may be different but the ballet's the same. There's nothing new. Like a fireworks display, these kinds of sequences differ in the quality of their choreography and their complication, timing, and their scope, and how much they get us to go *ooh ooh ooh*. Their greatness is mathematical, purely technical. And they're de rigueur for movies like this. Like McTiernan says, "I wanted the job, so this was my compromise."

So the second unit blows a lot of shit up, and then we can get on with the real movie. It's no surprise that after that sequence, the movie turns a corner and gets more interesting.

Even so, it's still surprising to hear McTiernan address the effects of being exposed to that much simulated gun violence so *directly* and so openly. And it's true: the great scene in *Die Hard* with all the shit blowing up and all the glass everywhere even gets echoed by the main character's line: "Glass? GLASS? Who gives a shit about GLASS?," and it's all sound and fury there too. But I don't think all this shooting signifies nothing either.

McTiernan's right that there's a difference between having people in front of those guns and not having them, but these giant scenes of ballistic violence still have an effect on those who watch them. I couldn't find a longer conversation with him about that "Or at least I thought I wasn't" in the middle of his riff, but it sure sounds to me like he takes some responsibility (if not as much as those who haven't approached the issue with his nuance) for how these explosions have echoed and keep echoing in the way spectacular violence has been normed.

It is a pornographic desire we're feeling. I mean, it's a pornographic desire I'm feeling, watching *Predator*. Maybe it always has been, or maybe when I'm watching it now it lights up the same obsessive visual centers of pleasure in my brain, and maybe they're rubbing up against something almost erotic, or at least completionist, a desire to move inexorably toward completion. All these bodies. All these guns. All these bodies holding guns and being killed by aliens. Could be I'm conflating my own sexual awakening with the movie's release: they happened right around the same time after all. I discovered pornography right around then, sometimes in the glove compartments of construction vehicles we'd raid on weekends. I also remember searching our whole house to find my father's porn, and occasionally finding it in dumpsters outside the apartment complex we lived in for a little while (why we were going through the dumpsters I don't remember, but I do remember finding a big cache of *Penthouse* magazines in one and secreting them off into the woods). I don't mind this desire; I've learned to live with it. It feels good, if a tad obsessive. How it operates in the brain: watching all these guns go off, all these explosions happening, all these pages flipping and showing me the same the same the same. I laugh and laugh: it's delightful, giddy. It's fucking nuts. All this force I'm seeing: how it makes me feel. It is weird how violent it all is, if somewhat abstractly, and how easily that disturbingness gets translated into laughter because what else are you going to do with it? Thinking about it—seeing it—doesn't make it less fun than the some fun I'm having tonight, but it complicates it all a little bit.

Maybe *Predator* didn't as obviously advertise the glory of guns to little kids as, say, *Rambo III* (truly a pornographic movie), but it successfully advertised the power of guns to me and my friends. Some twelve-year-olds may be able to parse the satirical nature of a film like this, but I wasn't up to it, or I didn't know I was. What I knew was that all these guns were awesome. That when things blew up I laughed and thrilled at all the wreckage. That we could blow shit up with guns and bombs. We knew how to do it, and we went ahead and did it. We subscribed to magazines like *Shotgun News*. We read the ridiculousness of *Soldier of Fortune*. We took it seriously. We bought weaponry when we could. My friend Chris—whose sister was killed, you'll remember—bought a lot of it. He bought guns, but he also bought crossbows and blowguns. I had shurikens (throwing stars) and a bunch of half-assed homemade katanas. We all had makeshift swords. We fired bottle rockets and Roman candles at each other. We bought as many fireworks as we could. We wanted more and more and more. We tried making our own napalm and nitroglycerin. We figured out how to make pipe bombs. We set them off usually in the woods. Mostly I've blocked out our pornographic mania for this stuff now, but I can feel myself in recalling these pieces getting a little of that old rush.

I mean, we didn't shoot *at* people. None of us, to my knowledge, ever killed or wounded anyone intentionally. And *Predator* wasn't the only current of the culture with this message, of course. Even *Predator* didn't have this message, though I didn't understand that then. All those action movies advertised the glory of explosives and the appeal of guns and shooting things to solve our problems, at least on-screen. Even if McTiernan won't cop to it, *Predator* does do that one task very, very well, at least for a while, until the movie turns into something else.

〈23〉

Some Fun

WE'RE BACK IN THE SIMULATED JUNGLE, and I do mean it's simulated jungle: the movie was filmed on two locations in Mexico, one right outside the tourist destination of Puerto Vallarta and the other around Palenque. Nobody realized when scouting the Puerto Vallarta location that the foliage there—while lush at the time they visited—is deciduous, so half the year it drops its leaves, which presents a problem if you're filming in that barren season. McTiernan points out how thin the jungle looked in a lot of the early scenes, but they'd already committed to it (it was close to where the producers had vacation homes) so they had to make artificial foliage, and even then, the so-called jungle wasn't nearly as jungly as desired. One review compared the foliage in some of the scenes to early winter in New England. Palenque brought real jungle to the later scenes, but wasn't as conveniently located for the comfort of the producers.

So back here in the simulated jungle, the guys are waiting, ready, and the creature falls into their trap—for a moment. In its escape the creature injures Poncho. And finally they see it through its camouflage. We are here, two-thirds of the way into the movie, and at 1:07 the creature is revealed for the first time, if not yet un-masked. It's a great reveal: the creature's face is iconic, with the metal facemask and the net-shrouded torso and the unforgettable dreadlocks. They're not actually dreadlocks—McTiernan didn't want to racialize the alien, he says—but they read that way to me at thirteen.

I've never understood the weird mesh shirt it wears, in the same way I don't understand the chain mail bikinis of fantasy illus-trators and movies like *Red Sonja*. I mean, I get the appeal: it looks hot/cool. But the utility eludes me.

Mac goes after the creature. Dutch is about to follow when Dillon says he'll go instead. He's redeemed in this moment and becomes one of our heroes not only by circumstance but also by action. Dutch tells him, "You can't win this, Dillon." To which he replies, "Maybe I can get even."

Here comes "Long Tall Sally" again—one more time, I want to remind you, this is the *only* song in the credits—as Mac pursues the thing into the jungle. Mac screams the lyrics to the gay man's song: "Long Tall Sally, she's built sweet. She got everything Uncle John needs. Oh baby. I'm gonna have me some fun."

I love this whole sequence, how the song gets increasingly his-trionic and deranged as he says it, dislocated from its original context in the movie. Desperate and crazed, Mac keeps repeating it—I'm gonna *have* me some fun; I'm gonna *have* me some fun; I'm gonna *have* me some fun; I'm gonna *have* me some fun—as he disappears into the jungle. It's hard not to be reminded of the insistence—to crazed exhaustion—of Men on the Internet that no way is Little Richard's "Long Tall Sally" a song about a man. These are things that we have to believe, I guess, or, as in that Rilke line, we must change our lives.

I'm gonna *have* me some fun.

Repetition to exhaustion and emptiness is one of the film's favorite effects, like with all that shooting and hitting nothing in the jungle. I am definitely having me some fun watching and rewatching *Predator*. If it wasn't fun, it wouldn't have been as popular as it was. All those explosions are sure some fun. Watching all these big boys is totally some fun. Watching Americans blow the shit out of everyone else is totally some fun (if you're American). But some fun doesn't translate into a work of art having the legacy that this fun does. That fun turns into desperation. If we tell ourselves how much fun we're having enough times, it eviscerates itself, doesn't it? All our guns, some fun, have no effect. All that tech: no effect. All those explosions: some fun, no effect; not on what really is hunting us.

I'm gonna *have* me some fun. It starts to feel like a self-command, doesn't it, how it keeps going, insistent.

What's hunting us is us, *Predator* tells us. It's a version of us— male, equipped, single-minded, armed, aggressive, showy, and powerful—but in all of these prized male qualities it's more amped than us. It kicks our asses. Or it kicks almost all our asses. All of our weaponry; all of our Second Amendment rights; all of our wars; and all of our interventions, covert and not, in other countries: Have these made us safer? (The answer, quite obviously, is no.)

I'm gonna have me some fun.

— I —
\24/

Predator vs. Ander

HAS ANYONE EVER TOLD YOU that *ander* means "other" in other languages? What other do you imagine yourself to be? How interesting do you think your life is to write about yourself this much? You look like you lost your mother. You only play at being bothered. You play at being a father: you don't teach your daughter what really matters. You don't even talk to your own father. You say more in here than you do to him in person when you see each other, which is once or twice a solar year. What part do you believe you still occupy in his life? Like him you've always been one to hold it in and when it comes out it comes out in anger. You're not gentle like you pretend to be. You're no hunter like you pretend to be. You are not marked or martyred by grief like you pretend. The Safeway and its shooting isn't yours. Neither was your babysitter's murder. You hijack tragedies to make yourself feel more important. Those hours you played in games do not constitute a second life; they do not count as grieving; they have no meaning. You know little better than others but act as if you do. I've noticed this is a common problem with men your age. From what I've seen it's not interesting to stare at a screen as you seem to often do. What does your obsession with my kind add up to? What do you see when you believe you see me? The movie doesn't mean what you think it means. It's an artificial thing. Little pudgy balding hetero, what do you know about the world of men? You do not speak for them. You hardly speak to them. You do not resemble them but believe you're like the boys. I feel you being threatened by them everywhere: how you hold your heat tells me more than you can know. Overhearing is not interacting. Nor is writing about what it is you see. Try touching something—somewhere—somehow. What do you know about the workings of the hidden world? You've made your little life and keep it safe. Even the coyote who carries off a stray in your front yard seems more alive than you: at least it registers what it wants and goes after it instinctively. Can you even imagine precarity the way I know the world to be? You talk a lot but constitute no threat to anything.

25

I See It. I See It.

I CAN STILL FEEL HOW WATCHING *Predator* as a teenager was a kind of desperation. It satisfied my desire to feel superior, to feel capable, to feel dominant. The movie gave me agency. It still does, to be honest. I insist on having me some fun. I could do a small bit of some of the stuff Dutch does in the movie, I told myself. I could make a booby trap. I could make a homemade bomb. I was maybe a third of Dutch's size and bulk, but still we wear him, don't we, watching the movie? He is us; his success is our success. He is a man. And even if we are not all men (some of us are boys, and some of us are something else), we are human, so we become him as we watch. Maybe just us boys or those who were once boys are the ones who become him when we watch. We wear our heroes, and eventually we wear them out. When we find out enough about them, they will let us down, when we find out about their desires and indiscretions, the way they played predator off-screen and did fucked-up shit, the way they get #metooed. But not by the end of the film. For the time being we wear Dutch as if we were in a powered man-suit, sort of like the character he plays in *The Terminator* and its sequels.

For the last half hour of *Predator*, though, we are still him, and we will triumph, we hope, if barely.

ON THEIR OWN NOW, Mac and Dillon finally both see it, the Predator, "out there past them trees," as Mac says. Dillon agrees. "I see it. I *see* it." Seeing it is the first step in understanding what it is. Seeing it lets you have at least a chance against it. Hard not to think here again of Monette, his partner Rog dying in a hospital room as he describes in *Borrowed Time*. It was published a year after *Predator* came out, and is his most acclaimed book, though he would win the National Book Award for 1992's *Becoming a Man: Half a Life Story.*

Most of Monette's bibliographies online do not include the novel *Predator.*

Why? Do they see it as a derivative work, something written for pay, not for art? It *is* that, of course, but that doesn't make it less a work of art, in the same way that though the movie *Predator* may well be a schlocky action movie, that doesn't make it any less a work of art, worthy of our attention. *Predator* was worthy of Monette's attention as his lover died. It should be worthy of ours, especially as the tenets of masculinity typified in the film remain a battleground in contemporary America. I wish I could say *Predator* and *Red Dawn* and *Commando* and all these movies felt like the artifacts of the past they are. But many men of my generation grew up on these. We ate them up. And here we are, in our thirties or our forties or our fifties, still trying to find a way to remain alive, or maybe I mean relevant. So many of us are angry.

A white male poet writes an essay about his eroding literary renown—and gets roasted for it, mostly rightly. I mean, he's not wrong to lament his waning fame, but read the room, dude, something that men of my generation are not great at doing. Another white male writer gets #metooed on Twitter as I'm rewatching the movie. Another can't *not* be an asshole to a younger emerging female writer he's paired with at a reading I attend. In fact, I'm here for the younger poet, as is most of the crowd: it's pretty obvious. But he's gotta pull rank and demands that he read last, and for longer. And he does, and it's pretty bad. What the fuck, dude? It's so obvious: it's hard to no longer be the star. He feels like he's being threatened. Maybe for the first time? I should say *we* feel like *we're* being threatened, because I am also a dude of a certain age. I know I occasionally exhibit this behavior, too, if I hope in a much more minor way. I preen and pose. I know how it goes. It's uncomfortable to see myself acting out these routines when I slip into them, and I do slip into them, and when I do I often see myself from outside myself as I'm being myself, or maybe as I'm being some more advanced version of these Internet Boy Trolls demonstrating how angry they get when someone plays with one of their toys, because they're boys, and because their toys have come to define them, and maybe my toys have come to define me too; maybe that's why I'm spending so many hours and years with my *Predator* movie and my Predator action figures and my Predator costume and my bullshit, and what the fuck, Ander? I want to say, when I see myself acting this way, and sometimes I even do, and break out of these well-learned grooves. I mean, I'm trying to break out of them.

These guys on-screen, though, are my dad's age almost exactly: I mean, at the time I watched it, they were my dad's age. Now when I watch it they're my age. When I watch them wane and die I think about my dad, hardly an action hero type but a good dad, and his mortality. He made some bad decisions too. We all do.

Then I think of myself.

I don't mean to be here an apologist for men. I don't think we need to apologize as a class. But so many of us are asses (or worse: predators), it's hard not to feel some rage at them, and then direct it at myself: What the fuck, men? What the fuck, us?

I want us at least to see ourselves.

I want to see that if the bad part of us can bleed, maybe we can kill it.

I'm not angry at masculinity exactly but I do have questions for it.

I had questions for Paul, too, so I took them to his archive. Why so little *Predator*, even in there? I found this in one of his journals: *Not having a credible career in Hollywood*. The novelization only merits a couple of mentions in his collected papers at the UCLA special collections archive, maybe because of a sentence I read in the contract for *Predator* that, unlike some of his other book contracts, is actually included in the archive. "We [the publisher] shall have the right but not the obligation to give you authorship credit on the jacket or cover of such novelization. . . . You acknowledge and agree that you are performing services in writing the manuscript under our direction, supervision and control." That tells you plenty about the relationship between the author and the novelization (vs. what this contract would look like if this were a "novel"). It was amended at his request to note that "we shall include a list of Author's credits in the novelization," so Monette did get his books listed in the front matter, including his other two novelizations.

I spent a good bit of time in the archives, and I found it a little overwhelming getting this close to Monette. Like all archives, his at UCLA is an intensely material space: it's 32.6 linear feet, consisting of sixty-four document boxes and seven flat boxes (when the finding aid was written anyway; the archive may have grown since then). I got credentialed and stored my bag and most of my gear in a locker. Put in a quarter and pocketed the key. I put in my requests for which boxes I wanted first. They ushered me back into a special reading room stacked floor to ceiling with beautifully bound books. The feeling I had—which is the feeling I always have in places like this—is a churchy feeling. I suppose it's reverence I'm talking about, but also a sense of intense authority, attention, and value. All of this—all of these people, and all of these resources—are devoted to physical collections, like the one I'm using. I wanted to faint, feeling all of that hush around me. It was beautiful, and it was privilege, and it was isolation all at once. It was the war and the warrior, Monette might have said, and if he could have imagined the disconnect between all of this propriety and proprietariness and all of that energy and beautiful attention directed at pages in which he is marking down the dick size of a bunch of dudes. Well, I think he would have been entertained. Perhaps he was, thinking of his own passing.

But either way, these were *his* pages I was touching, if I was allowed to touch them without the requisite white archival gloves. In fact, I did touch the pages sneakily when the archivists were not in the room. I rubbed my fingers along them, wondering. I didn't feel any electricity, not really, or if I did, it was all mine that I'd brought into the room. I was fascinated by one folder from the collection: it consisted only of ten 5.25-inch floppy disks. What was on them? No one knows. They had not been accessed. I mean, good luck accessing them anyway. Floppy disks may last a decade or two if you're lucky, but they are not media made for long-term storage. I asked if they had equipment to read them, but was told that they did not. Of course they didn't. You'd have to bring in some old-school tech nerds who collect this stuff and still maintain machines in order to get them read. And even if they were readable, who knows what would be on them anyway? Most have glossy red sleeves reading *Custom packaged for Computerland. We know small computers.* The other read *Nashua. Professional Magnetic Media.* Two were Datalife by Verbatim. They each had a bunch of labels: *Winter #3*; *Wave, 30something* (I'm pretty sure: it's hard to read the handwriting); *Havana 67-140*; *Time 448-509*; *Pau. Journals. Time 7-0139. Hitch*; *Wave 1, 2*; *Maids2, Poems 2*; *Whoopie 2, Poems 1*; *Winter Spring 2*; *Tears / Outline.* The last read, most tantalizingly, *No Secrets #2.*

I still have diskettes like this. I got rid of almost all of mine, I mean, besides the ones the Secret Service task force confiscated. I didn't have much left. When they raided my dorm room they took it all, all of anything that might remotely be considered evidence of computer crime. They took some pornographic magazines I had collected (probably for their own uses, I'd imagine: what could they be evidence of except my perversion?). They even took my Wilson Phillips CD. Accidentally? Or did they grab whatever looked interesting to them, knowing that a seventeen-year-old who'd had his dorm room raided by a task force was in no position to complain about what they'd taken of his shit. Was someone's kid into Wilson Phillips and figured it would never be missed? Or did the agent think he was doing me a favor by eliminating it from my collection?

I still have a few of my old disks, though, thanks to my dad, who kept those boxes. They wouldn't have been with me at school, and are now part of my dad's garage archives of all my old shit. I open up the case for the original *Bard's Tale* for MS-DOS and finger the diskettes. They retain a certain amount of totemic power for me, how much of a world even these relatively rudimentary games could open up for me then. I imagine this is much how some aficionados feel about their vinyl collections (and I do fetishize the LP a little bit, but that was never my primary music media: most of my memories are set to the early years of CDs).

I even still have the *Bard's Tale Clue Book*, a booklet that had the maps of all the dungeons and some suggestions for how to solve them, which was the only way I was able to complete the game. In my defense, some of the dungeons were intensely difficult and impossible to map, because you'd get teleported or spun around, and this was before games like this came with mapping features. I can even see my own attempts to hand-map some of the dungeons, including the first one, "The Sewer" ("we are in a muck-drenched stinking sewer, and the beasts and blackguards who attack us here are too numerous to be described," the accompanying journal goes: I think the book is supposed to be a journal of another adventuring party who had tried to complete the quests and perished right before the end—or something). Later, I've marked

the location of a crystal golem in Kylearan's Tower, and I reproduced some meaningful lines of a bad poem uttered by a "magic
mouth" (I don't remember what this is). I've chucked much of the
rest of the artifacts of my time spent in those days, but for some
reason these scraps remain. I don't imagine that I'll have an archive at a place as prestigious as Monette's at UCLA, but I do like
to imagine future scholars encountering some of these sage tidbits
in the bowels of one box or another.

Oh, I meant to clarify before, because it does matter: you spell
disk (short for *diskette*) with a *k* when you're talking about magnetic media; you use a *c* for optical media, so a *disc* is a CD-ROM
or a Blu-ray, for instance; a *disk* is magnetic, like a hard drive or a
floppy disk. Typing this ridiculousness, I can imagine Blain—or
Monette for that matter—making a joke about hard and floppy
dicks. I will always contain my adolescent self.

All Monette's mentions of time on the labels were hard for
me to ignore, and to not wonder what might have been on these
disks, and how time changes when you or someone you love is in
the middle of a crisis that they and you may not see the end of.
Maybe these disks still hold information that could be accessible.
Or perhaps they have degraded over time. One diskette's sleeve
read *Timeless Warranty*.

I suggested to the archivists that they needed to get the tech
to extract these data, if data still remained, as soon as possible. I
told them—and they knew, but maybe didn't want to have to face
it—that magnetic diskettes were not meant to last. Someone put a
note in a file. Anything could be on there! I said. I requested the
materials from the diskettes, should they be able to extract them.

In another world, I imagined my toting in my old 80386 Gateway
2000—surely long since discarded from whatever evidence locker
they kept on me—and firing up those disks to crack the secrets of
Monette's archives. But in this world I put in a request and didn't
expect to hear back, probably ever. Monette mattered enough to
have an archive, but he didn't merit that kind of digital forensics:

that would be expensive and annoying. How important could a bunch of crap on floppy disks be?

Monette's archive contained a lot of selves, including his adolescent ones. I zeroed in on the years when he may have been working on *Predator*, and here are the only mentions of that work. First, shortly before Rog's death:

> The tablet was in place, beautiful and heartbreaking. . . . It *is* like another funeral, sealing of the tomb. But it came out just like I wanted it.

> 3/21 3AM
> I can't even remember the last 3 days but I—I got *Predator* off to Berkley [the publisher of *Predator*] + finished the *Dreaming Poem*, then took the 3rd page apart on Thursday night to make it better.

Many more pages are spent on the kinks and physical appearances of various dudes ("Pete: Australian, 7½ thick, medical, hot tub, hairy"). But later he writes, "What does it mean that I didn't die?"

Predator shows up in banal ways over the course of a couple of other journals. On August 25, Paul's "working on *Predator*. Alfred came over tonight," then below there's a quote from Sanford Schwartz, whoever that is, then the very next journal entry is dated October 30, and begins "Roger died on the 22nd at 6 o'clock in the morning. I keep forgetting the date." Things break down for a few pages, and there are many gaps. Life goes on, it seems. Fragments of poems start appearing with regularity, then full drafts with edits. A few pages later, here's a draft of Rog's epitaph. Journal entries become more frequent again. The following January, he writes, "In line for *Platoon*. Fred came by today and I readied things for the accountant." In February, "I'm lying in the bed where Rog lay last March, just the night before the blindness began. . . . Dad took the *Predator* leaflet out to the pool to show everybody. How Rog would

have loved that." More poems, then in March, "I was just thinking, thinking about *Predator*, on p40 of the page proofs, about the
[unreadable: my best guess is "lifting"] feeling during *Scarface*
[which he also novelized], all that loneliness that went with being
attached, with saying it here and there." On June 14th, 1987: "This is
our kind of day, darling. Cool and breeze w/ bright sun, very very
summer. *Predator* and dinner last night w/Sam, Friday stayed in,
week of looking clearly and closely at me."

When I look at the photographs I took of the pages in Monette's
archive, the thing I notice is how often the shadow of my phone,
the agent of my photography, appears. Some pages I managed to
prop up to avoid this effect, but still there I am, casting my crappy
shadow all over all that remains of Monette. This makes me more
than a little uncomfortable.

Another page I photographed for unknown reasons appears to
be some kind of piece of literary criticism:

> The situation of these characters is ultimately the situation of
> Thomas himself. Grappling with the inexorable dualities, he
> is by turns the observer and the participant, the self and the
> other; shuttling between the observatory and the street, his ex-
> perience is "inseparablement vecue et ecrite." Fundamentally,
> however, he is the witness, the one who remains to tell the
> story—much as we all, for the time—remain—reaching through
> language to silence.

I don't remember why I photographed this particular page, since I
don't know who Thomas is or what work is being discussed, but
that last bit resonates beautifully.

I flick through to another image in my files that resolves the
question: the thesis was not Monette's but Rog's, his PhD thesis
in comparative literature from Harvard. It's a beautiful little mis-
direction, thinking these words were Paul's when they were Rog's.
From *Predator*: "You could no longer tell whose blood was whose."

Of course, Monette did die, as did Rog. We all will. Some of us will be left and remembered as long as there are those who care enough about us to remember us. Our data may outlive us. Maybe our notes and journals will outlive us. Or the games we played and the records of how we played them. How many achievements did we unlock? How many trophies did we earn in *The Outer Worlds*? How did my digital marriage to Maru go in *Stardew Valley*? What was the final sum of all the games I played? The tally of the number of times I watched *Predator* and the evidence of what, if anything, or what—of everything—it did to me?

Walking by the new refrigerator after midnight on my way to bed, the motion detector lights up on the water dispenser. It's automatic, but it's still hard for me not to appreciate its noticing my presence and my passage.

⟨26⟩

That First-Person Feeling

WHILE SEEING THE ALIEN is a promising development, seeing it is not enough. The Predator is still far stronger than they are. It has so many advantages. By the time Mac thinks he has the alien, it has him instead. We see the laser sight of its cool-ass shoulder cannon on Mac's arm, and then he's done. He turns to face the thing. His head explodes. The shot is from behind the head, obviously a prop head, but a convincing effect, as the shot comes from the front and blows right through the skull. Blood and brain matter flower back toward us and coat the camera in red. It's supergross if by this point you're not inured to it. I am, of course, inured to it. You are, too, if you made it this far in. The movie's gore is part of the point, the thrill, and the more visceral they could make it the better: "More blood!" Another shot of his just-shot body as it twitches drives home the point. We watch the laser sight recede, and we see the camouflaged alien stand atop him for a moment then stride away to deal with Dillon. Mac's leg fucking twitches six times as the creature recedes. That will be the last we'll see of Mac, and the movie's poorer for his loss. Now none of those who remain have any real bond. They will be pursued.

Anna stoops to pick up Poncho's gun. Dutch tells her, "Don't. Leave it. It didn't kill you because you weren't armed: no sport." It's unclear how Dutch knows this is the honor code of the beast. For all we know, it only kills men, understandably. After all, so far it has only killed men: the Green Berets, men in Anna's community, the men in Dutch's party: "so many man, so much killed." Even in 1987, one might not blame it. It's easy to see how men and following them have led us to where we are: in a world on the brink of nuclear war, a world that's rapidly and inexorably getting hotter (I text the "it only comes in the hottest years" GIF to a friend who asked me, "How's that 115 degrees treating you?"), and more and more unequal, and increasingly warlike. I consult a list of "wars involving the United States" and, citing only those from the end of World War II to the release of *Predator*: the Korean War, the Laotian Civil War, the Lebanon crisis, the Bay of Pigs invasion, the Simba rebellion, the Vietnam War, the communist insurgency in Thailand, the Korean DMZ conflict, the Dominican Civil War, the insurgency in Bolivia, the Cambodian Civil War, the war in South Zaire, the Gulf of Sidra encounter, the multinational intervention in Lebanon, the invasion of Grenada, action in the Gulf of Sidra, the bombing of Libya, and the Tanker War, not to mention the Cold War that we're right in the middle of in 1987. This is not a great record for human men—and that's just *American* men. We're not even getting into the rest of the world's men! Perhaps the Predator is here to thin the ranks of all these predators, all these men who want to go to war and blow the earth to hell?

We will find out in the second movie that Dutch is right, that the Predator does have an honor code, and it will not, unlike us, attack the unarmed or the vulnerable. But in 1987 we still weren't sure, even if Dutch was. And this leads us to another iconic death scene.

We cut back to Dillon, who now realizes Mac is dead, as he stands on the edge of a clearing, looking up for the Predator. He sees it as it sees him (its eyes light up with a yellow glow, which would seem to be a competitive disadvantage) and, in slow motion, raises one of his guns to fire. He begins to shoot as he is hit.

Of the many fingers on many triggers *Predator* shows us, this one might be the most unforgettable. It's shocking watching it still firing, severed from his body. The monster's shot Dillon's forearm off with its laser and there it is, still shooting, unattached, as it fires senselessly along the jungle floor. That's how *pissed* it is, how *man* it is, how human it is, how unthinking, how obsessive. It fires and fires and fires.

You can kill the man, but even then he'll fire the gun. It doesn't even take a brain! Charlton Heston says you can pry it from his cold dead hands, which I guess we'll have to do in a few. If we didn't get the point from the Great Laying Waste to the Jungle earlier, it's pretty obvious now. After their dazzling raid of the outmatched guerrilla camp, every other shot they fire in the film (except for the one that wounds the thing) misses the mark but makes the point.

Compare to another shot in *True Lies*, another Schwarzenegger action epic, this one from 1994. The film is only pretty good. I've only seen it four or five times. Directed by James Cameron, who had previously directed *Piranha II*, *The Terminator*, *Aliens*, *The Abyss*, and *Terminator 2* (at least three of these are stone-cold classics) and would go on to make *Titanic* and *Avatar*, *True Lies* has that emptiness I find at the heart of most action movies. Its characters are one-dimensional. They're funny—they make jokes—but they don't feel alive. No one seems to be talking to anyone else: they're only reading lines. As such the film's violence has a gleeful meaninglessness. It does have some awesome shots, however, including one in which Jamie Lee Curtis, who plays the unsuspecting wife of Schwarzenegger's secret superspy character, is handed an Uzi to defend herself, but she doesn't know how to shoot it. As she sprays bullets vaguely in the direction of the bad guys, she loses control of it and it leaves her hands, pinwheeling down a flight of stairs, still firing, pinwheeling, hitting another stair and firing, and it kills at least a dozen bad guys who are menacing her and her husband, all without her actually having her finger on the trigger and having to reckon with the responsibility of killing. We get a close-up of her "whoopsie!" face right after. Guns don't fucking kill people, my neighbor's bumper sticker tells me. I don't think McTiernan believes this, but Cameron does.

Like the tumbling Uzi, this shooting arm is so grotesque, it's hard not to laugh at it, if only because that's the most easily available emotional response. How else are we supposed to feel? It's so over the top and fucked up. It's brilliant. Dillon screams. The camera lingers on his disconnected arm. The arm still pulses with simulated blood, the finger twitching on the trigger, bullets flying: I count seventeen of them, none of which are more than roughly in the direction of his target. Who knows what, if anything, they hit. Somehow he raises his other gun in his other hand, the one still attached to his dying body, to fire at the Predator left-handed, but it gets to him first and hoists him into the air on the end of a bladed fist. He screams again, shooting and dying: his last act.

WITH MAC AND DILLON GONE, the team is down to four. Dutch and Poncho and Anna and Billy all hear the screams. Dutch and Poncho and Anna hurry into the jungle. Billy will not go; he turns and throws his gun definitely into the river. He begins to disrobe— because of hotness reasons I imagine (both his physical form and the ambient temperature)—and face his death. His crazed stare remains in my memory. He's a crazy dude—the character but also the actor, Sonny Landham. McTiernan reports that the insurance company required them to hire a bodyguard for Landham when he was cast as Billy. The bodyguard was not to protect Billy from others, but to protect others from *him*.

Still, dude has a compelling presence on-screen. Some imagined he might be the third *Predator* star to make a go of it in national politics, as he ran an independent campaign for the Kentucky governor's office. That failed, then he ran for senate against Mitch

McConnell in 2008 as a Libertarian. It was an unhinged campaign, even for Kentucky, as he repeatedly called for "genocide" against Arabs (whom he referred to as "camel-dung shovelers," "camel jockeys," and "rag-heads"). Shortly after this outburst the Kentucky Libertarian Party voted to withdraw his nomination, which tells you something. He was also convicted of making threatening and obscene phone calls to his wife and jailed for three years before being released on appeal. She claimed he once shot a pistol past her head. He was a bad, bad drunk. He died in 2017 as I rewatched and rewatched *Predator*.

Billy's might be the most famous death in the movie, even if it's off-screen, because unlike the others it asks a question: Why does it go down this way? Why does he chuck his radio and gun and carve a line across his chest with a huge knife and wait for the predator atop a massive log over a river? Has he, as Monette told us, having his extrasensory perception, concluded that he has no chance against the alien and wants to buy some time for his comrades to escape? We heard Billy tell us earlier, after all, that "we're all gonna die." Is he choosing the most honorable death of the ones available to him? Or has he figured it's his destiny to meet the creature one-on-one in hand-to-hand combat, so that he ritualistically wounds himself to show his willingness and to set the terms of the engagement: no guns, just men with blades? We've already seen the team outgunned and outcamouflaged and outtrapped and outwitted in every way imaginable, so perhaps he feels this is his best or only chance.

In the 1985 script Billy (then called Miguel) never confronts the creature and makes it to the end. In the 1987 script he dies. We're told "Taking another dap of paint [from his GREASE-PAINT TIN, not his own blood] he makes a SYMBOL on his bare skin. . . . Staring outward, as if in a trance, he begins a low CHANT. . . . Billy stands at the foot of the bridge, knife raised, waiting, accepting his oncoming destiny." He then dies off-screen. The novelization tells us, "A Sioux defending his ancestors died the noblest death of all. . . . Billy was as beyond the earth now as the alien."

None of these is completely satisfying, because Billy's backstory has always been pretty thin. The novel *almost* seems to know this, telling us, "The alien had taken him in a flash, its weapon slicing through the Indian's jugular and then zigzagging down his chest and belly like a mockery of some tribal blessing," missing the irony of its own shallow treatment of Billy's Indianness.

In the movie he cuts himself; I can't tell if it's a symbol or not. He makes no chant. He just fights and screams and dies.

So I'm just not sure. It won't resolve.

I mean, I see some of the potential whys, but why don't we *see* him die? This film's reveled in showing us literally everyone else's bloody end and just how brutal it was. It'd be easy enough to chalk it up to the shooting schedule or the budget, since you can't show everything all the time, but his death is even off-screen in the final script. I've asked the internet, and there's plenty of discussion about the question, dudes on forums explaining to each other what the character would have done, but nothing from anyone involved. Is this accidental erasure, not even giving the Native American character a filmed death scene? Or does it honor him, not having to see him gutted? Or is it just a failure of imagination?

I stare at the screen for answers, but none come. He bleeds off-screen, but there's no time to know.

Suddenly the creature's on the rest of them! It kills Poncho with a shot to the head. Again Dutch prevents Anna from picking up a gun and instead fires his own massive weapon toward the tree harboring the creature, which gets blown apart. I'm no botanist, but foliage in this film does not fare well.

WITH THIRTY MINUTES LEFT IN THE FILM, Dutch is finally about to be alone. Wounded, he yells at Anna to "get to da choppa," another line from the movie I hear quoted with regularity among men. She bolts into the forest, unarmed. Dutch takes off into the forest wearing what I suppose we have to call a shirt, but covers less than a tank top. Maybe it's a tactical tank top. I think that's what it's meant to be, but what point it has I have no idea. The gaze in this movie is male, but it sure spends a lot of time looking at men. It may be that I am not hard-core enough to understand.

He slides off the edge of a cliff and into a river, then over a waterfall, and here we're moving toward one of the things you have to swallow to move along in the movie's fantasy: he drags himself out of the mud, nearly naked, smeared in mud, pursued by the Predator, cornered, and as it emerges from the water and shakes its dreadlocks, we see—he sees—and in its face we see *it* see—that it cannot see Dutch, smeared head to toe with the mud as he is. It only sees heat, and the mud obscures his heat.

The obvious complaint is that this would work maybe a minute or two only before the body heat warms through the mud, and besides aren't we in a jungle that's got to be hotter than a body? But you can't focus too much on these questions. I have to leap along. I get the idea: I don't want *that* much realism in my alien battle horror war movie anyway. It sees some kind of heat moving—a rat crawling on a log, maybe?—and blasts it (so much for not killing unarmed creatures), showering the mud-smeared Schwarzenegger with sparks. That's the point of the shot anyhow, and of so many of these shots in this movie and others: to get to the one shot you want, the beautiful one, and this is one of the great ones. I've been showered in sparks from, say, fireworks, not an alien weapon, and it does sting. We watch him grimace a little. As it looks around and walks away, Dutch sighs in relief. He looks at the mud on his body, and so begins his plan to fight back.

As it turns out the Predator didn't kill the rat, or whatever it is. It squeals and runs away. Run, rat, run! So now the odds are even, or closer to even. A montage of shirtless, homemade, jungle booby-trapping ensues. If the Predator were looking now, it would see him, the mud having dried and largely smeared off. His wounds would be fresh and hot in the heat-light of the thing.

Schwarzenegger's body gleams in the light like a beautiful tool. He lifts. He's strong. Covered in mud, he's become part of the jungle. It's not blackface, but the effect is visually similar, emphasizing the whites of his eyes.

Cut to the Predator who's pulled the skull and spinal column from, I think, Billy, though it may have been Poncho. It's hard to tell: we all look so similar when skinned and bled. It roars and cleans the human remainder from the bone. It's gross. I think of taxidermy again and all those eviscerated creatures in the Wildlife Museum across town. And here's Dutch still in the montage, with a fire he's made. He's bending a branch. He flex. He sex. He's made a makeshift bow. Our bro. He's made, I guess, some kind of flash grenade with leaves and the remaining gunpowder from one of his shells that were maybe strapped to his technical tank top. The script describes this like so:

> Finally, using several sections of BAMBOO of differing diameters, he fashions a crude, anti-personnel SPEAR-BOMB, a BANG-STICK like weapon, using the sharpened TONGUE from his belt buckle for a FIRING PIN and a 40MM GRENADE from his belt pouch as an explosive charge.

Reading those capitalized words has the EXPLOSIVE EXCITED EFFECT on me that was probably intended, and that helps to soundtrack the way it may have felt writing it. It gets a rise out of me reading it, even if I recognize the BLUNT STUPIDITY of its CALLS to MANHOOD.

Flash back to Predator, with its weird mesh covering its skin and a bunch of what I think are skulls attached to it. He looks ready to go out to a goth club. The Predator continues its preparation, as we see all the SKULLS of the BEINGS it's KILLED in its menagerie, much of which it carries on it. We get no shots of the ship in this film (wait till the sequel for that). I'll stop with the CAPS even though I ENJOY it. I bet it's DISTRACTING.

The thing considers the skull, as if to say, "Alas, poor Yorick" or "What's up with all these men I hunt?"

THE THING THAT SAVES HIM—that saves Dutch, and by extension us, Americans, men, well, *me*, is whom I'm really talking about, because when Dutch kills the thing, it's me who kills the thing on some level: it's all of us killing the thing on some level. But also I mean us, humans: we save us, at least in the movie we do. And the part of us that saves us is not brute strength or aggressiveness or fractiousness or technological superiority or dickishness or sheer sexual tyrannosaurin but ingenuity. What do all these men with all these guns amount to, after all? Sound and fury: great sound. Great fury. Big men. Big bodies. All that's gone. A bunch of skulls and skin and thousands of shell casings in the jungle. We're left with one beautiful man, stripped of his team and nearly all of his gear, against a technologically and physically superior foe.

I dunno. My beefy, hardass, high school football coach Jim Luoma would probably tell me that what carries the day is *grit*, or maybe effort, the kind you're supposed to give 110 percent of, or maybe perspiration, but I don't think so. I think it's inspiration, the moment he sees what it sees and doesn't see, and how we can use that to our advantage. That's the hopeful message of the film. That once we see what our adversary can and cannot see, we can start to fight it. I mean, otherwise, everybody dies: the team, sure, all these hard and gleaming guys with long histories of military kickassery. But also the whole guerrilla camp, basically (and for nothing), and also Hopper and his men, and surely hundreds if not thousands of other men, hunted and killed by the "Demonio," as Anna's village calls it, and who knows how long these things have hunted us? (This is a question explored to entertaining effect in the sequels.)

I mean, from a practical standpoint, after all this damage, at this point, what does it matter if Dutch kills the Predator or the Predator kills Dutch? If the creature wins, it goes back into space with a really good skull trophy for its case and leaves the rest of us alone. If Dutch wins, it's a win for earth and earthly men, but so much has been lost already. If we assume the thing's a one-off, then maybe a win for us saves the world. But if there's one, there's going to be another sooner or later. If I watched the movie with my economist father, he'd pause and remind me that everything that's transpired is all sunk cost and how we shouldn't let these affect our decision making. Dad, I get it: I know you're right, but being right doesn't change the way I feel, how the movie's made me feel. It's the emotional/art logic that's keeping us going: no way can we stop now.

Even so, it's refreshing to be reminded that, though we consider ourselves apex predators with our Big Guns and our Big Cars and our Big Feels, first, most of us aren't (go to Costco or Culver's or Cabela's to be reminded of our vulnerability), and second, we are ill suited for the role. We're soft. Most of us are safe in one way or another. We have no shells. (Maybe this is why we have to outfit ourselves in "tactical gear" and big chunky SUVs?) Our ability to see and sense is more limited than that of most fauna on this planet. Maybe let's embrace the thrill in being the hunted too.

We are also the hunted in our lives, in different ways, which is what we're trying to protect ourselves against by buying and yelling and arming. Violence and mass shootings plague us. Most of us have some near connection to one or more communities that have been impacted by violence. For me it's Gabrielle Giffords and the Safeway shooting. It was my babysitter. It was the neighbor who blew his face off. For you it might be Sandy Hook or any of the long list of other shootings or murders, some famous, some not.

IN 2018, after the latest in a string of mass shootings nationally, including many on university campuses, I attend an active shooter response training workshop presented to the English Department at my workplace. I don't really expect to get much out of the experience, but we're one dumb Arizona law away from allowing guns on campus anyway, which I joke would change the tenor of my creative writing workshops. It's an afternoon in one of the seminar rooms, and I go because I'm curious, and it is a curious event.

The police captain running the workshop tries to reassure us: "They almost always announce it on social media" and "most of the 190 active shooter incidents are in rural communities. The motive is usually some combination of anger, revenge, ideology, and untreated mental illness." "Now we have rifles on the rooftops during football games or when big events happen," he tells us. "There are two teams we have set up in contingency: the hunting team and the evacuation team. The hunting team: we're hunting this person. By the way, these active shooters are always guys."

I know, a few counterexamples suggest themselves: Tashfeen Malik (San Bernardino, 2015), Jennifer San Marco (Goleta, Calif., 2016), Brenda Spencer (Cleveland, 1979), Amy Bishop (University of Alabama, 2010), Laurie Dann (Winnetka, Ill., 1988), Latina Williams (Baton Rouge, 2008), Snochia Moseley (Aberdeen, Md., 2018), Yvonne Hiller (Philadelphia, 2010), and that about covers recent history. Is it easier to know "it's always guys"? Or as a guy, what am I meant to do with that fact? I mean, of course it's always guys. Who else would it be? Who else has no time to bleed?

He continues: "As for you, you run or escape if possible. Fight only as a last resort. Make sure that when you walk into a building you know where the stairs are. This is hide-and-seek quite frankly. You're just playing hide-and-seek and run. Turn off your cell phone ringer, obviously. In a pinch, if you have one of these over-the-door hinges on your door, like we have in this room, you tie a belt around it and it'll slow him down. What you want is to slow him down, to make him find someone else. That's the goal. You don't want to stop him. Slow him down. Make it slightly harder for him to get you. And whatever you do—throw items, improvise weapons, yell—you want to commit to your actions. These situations are unpredictable. They evolve quickly. They are dynamic."

None of this is reassuring. I find my attention slipping to the

promo sheet for the DMX Run 10 X Predator, a new shoe from
Reebok that a friend emailed me an hour earlier. I bring it up on
my laptop as I listen:

> Combing [sic] elements from the original 1987 Predator film
> and its latest combat mission, this cinematic collectible takes a
> new spin on the veteran DMX Run 10. . . . It arrives in custom
> packaging inspired by the Predator's thermal-imaging vision.

The shoes retail for $200. If run we must, then I guess I ought
to be prepared. I consider ordering a pair, but the only sizes remaining on the website are: 4, 5, 5.5, 6.5, 8, 8.5, and 10, all of which
would be too small.

Also from the website:

> Mimicking the Predator's invisibility cloak is a shimmering
> camouflage material designed on the upper. A bold yellow
> iconic vector logo peers from outside the tongue and eerie di-
> rections in the creature's natural language can be found on the
> inside. As a nod to covert operations, glow-in-the-dark graph-
> ics light up the shoe.

I'm not sure whoever wrote the copy understands or perhaps
has ever seen the film. The Predator's visits to earth are not combat missions. And even if they were, wouldn't you want your shoe,
if nodding to covert missions, *not* to glow while running covertly
at night?

After attending the presentation, it's not hard to be appointed
to the Active Shooter Response Committee, which is a distinction
I'm not putting on my CV, and I'm not really sure what our collective work entails except to listen to the captain's thoughts on men
and think about what best to do with our belts. As part of my work
on the committee, I watch a UA police department active shooter
simulation video that claims to model what would happen in the

case of an active shooter on campus. It's shot on location in the Student Union and across campus, with students as volunteers, and as such it's genuinely unsettling: here's the corridor where I get my Chick-fil-A, extra pickle, extra mayo. Here's the stairs that lead to the graduating MFA students' convocation. These people fleeing are students I sometimes see. And here's a trench-coated white guy with a disaffected look. Oh, I get it: he's the shooter in this simulation. Of course he gets taken down eventually.

HERE'S A THING I never understood from *Predator*: At 1:26 we flip back to the Predator as it runs its three-dot targeting light along its savage-looking BLADES.

I'm SORRY! It sounds both super COOL and DUMB to write this, and both effects resonate in me at once: How SWEET are its BLADES? How great are these sculpts that make for such a COOL SUIT? And how dumb is this to have spent a decade or more watching this kind of dumb movie? At any rate, it's only from the script that I understand what this scene is supposed to mean: "Raising in one hand his weapon, in the other a U-shaped SHARPENING DEVICE. As he passes the weapon through the device, it FLASHES into life, a deep, HARMONIC HUM emitted as the blade glows with energy, growing hotter, hotter and HOTTER with each stroke."

One might register some erotic feelings, reading this. And this: "He draws the blade now WHITE-HOT through the device for the last stroke. He lifts it, testing its balance, the WHITE-HOT blade illuminating his alien face."

And here he is, Dutch, newly slathered in fresh wet mud and ready—at last—to fight it on his terms. He screams out to the thing. He has its attention.

I LOVE HOW WHEN you spend a ton of time focusing on one thing, it starts to resonate with the rest of the world. I know a lot of what I see in *Predator* is in *Predator*, and a lot of what I see in *Predator* is in me, but it's also a filter for the world: there's so much of the world that made *Predator* in *Predator*. Dillon is a character in *Predator*. Dillon is the manufacturer of the Aero M-134D Minigun. I'm not a character in *Predator*, but Predator is a character in me. The more I see those skulls the more I flip back to Tucson's International Wildlife Museum and the work of all those men who killed all those things whose skulls and bones and sometimes fur and skin are preserved and collected there. For what? I mean, what really?

The Predator Masters internet hunting club (website slogan: "Hunting the Hunter"—how *Predator*!) hosted their yearly convention there a few years ago. I went on their website to see if the Predator Masters were all dudes. The answer, unsurprisingly, is yes. Their administration page lists sixteen: Jason El Paso, 220_Swift, Jeff Mock, Matt1953, Infidel 762, Stu Farish, Jack Roberts, Kerry Carver, SnowmanMo, Redfrog, SteveM, reb8600, OldTurtle. This includes (collects) the dead: Jack Roberts, SteveM, and OldTurtle are listed as deceased. I looked at every photo, and count only four women among the (small) crowds at their 2019 convention.

I come from hunting country, and am not philosophically or morally opposed to hunting. I don't believe the only real hunting is hunting men, as Ventura told us when he was governor. But I think you ought to be obliged to eat what you kill and to treat the experience with the respect that a life lost deserves. When the Predator Masters come to town for a convention, they don't only hobnob about gear and tactics and strut and posture in front of each other. As the *Tucson Daily Star* reported, they also go on hunts in the surrounding area. The previous year they shot and killed and left to decay at least forty coyotes on one of their hunts. They didn't shoot the animals for meat. They didn't take their skins. They reportedly used electronic calls that sounded "like coyote pups calling for their mothers, or a rabbit in distress" and then shot the coyotes when they came close. They also often shoot "bobcats, gray foxes . . . raccoons, ringtail cats and coatimundis." They—and similar groups—were part of other wildlife-killing contests in

Arizona in the last few years, including the World Championship Coyote Calling Contest, Santa Slay Coyote Calling Tournament, Big O Coyote Hunt, Tonopah Valley Future Farmers of America Alumni Coyote Hunt, Arizona Coyote Calling Championship, Arizona Predator Callers Multi-Club Hunt, Another Varmint Tournament (judged, I need to tell you, by "Armando Navarrete" and someone who calls himself "Tactical Cody"; their flyer also tells contestants, "Don't soak your coyote in water because it will not be counted"—since the contest is judged by weight), South Eastern Arizona Coyote Calling Challenge, Ray Evridge Memorial Disabled Veterans Predator Hunt, Antelope Eaters Hunt, and the Save a Fawn Hunt. The prizes are cash and guns, including an AR-15.

27

A Blue Ring Seen through Water

I WATCH *PREDATOR* every night to help me sleep. It doesn't work, so I repeat. To say I'm still watching the film closely isn't exact enough. I mean, I watch the movie frame by frame, so slowly it's no longer a movie but film, happy illusion of the form, the frames' elision that we perceive as motion. It's totally kickass, of course, at full speed, but, seen as slowly as this, it opens differently: it ain't just guns and fun. One by one through twenty-four frames per second it's often tedium: action film gone ambient. As a result I find beauty leaking around a tree in an establishing shot. Then pyro light explodes in lines, telling us something about physics, cause and effect, and the only thing that matters is how it looks. Something happens and keeps on happening and won't stop until I do or the movie ends or I realize what it is I'm watching and assert control. Unexpected shots abound, inaccessible to all but the most obsessive viewer. The wipe that clears the screen between bits of the Predator's POV looks like an ellipse of blue light seen through dark green water. It's an opening you might use to speak to an oracle. Or an open eye. A wishing well seen from underneath, down in it, looking out. But the more I look at it, the more

I see a reflection of a body in the center of the shot, something in there staring right back at me, and I wonder what portal I may have opened accidentally by calling the wrong god's name. Is that me in *Predator*? Better: What of me is *not* in *Predator*? I could spend a life down here. For you it takes three-hundredths of a second.

HERE'S ANOTHER SHOT I can't stop looking at: the creature, having been lured into the trap laid by Dutch, moves slowly along the length of giant tree that is broken in half and parallel to the ground. The crew had to build this tree. There was nothing like it in the jungle where they were filming. It was "made by a team of about fifty over two weeks," McTiernan tells us in the commentary track. We see the creature in relief against the fires Dutch has set in the background. Going frame to frame there's one moment as the fires flicker in which the slope of the creature's head and neck—seen through its camouflage effect—is mirrored almost exactly by the path of flame at the right. It's perfect: I'd love to show you it. It's at 1:28:23 if you're going frame by frame at home. But what I want to know is how accidentally this shot was made. How much can you shape the pyro (probably a lot: we tame fire as it suits our needs), and did someone plan it this way (probably not but maybe): to reveal a poetry? The eye seeks similarity. Watching the film this way—shot by shot and frame by frame, in slow motion—all the accidents seem inevitable. This is, I guess, the effect of art, or my willingness to believe and find myself in film. I believe that if I look at it hard enough the screen will fade and I will see myself and then the culture that made me, to the degree it did. In fact, a bit right from center—under the flame's tentacular curl reaching out from the left—I stare at it and seem to find a face. Even the background vines echo the creature's curls and curves.

Our phones and digital cameras are trained to find the face and focus on it: it's what the machines believe we want (because we said we did): to see ourselves in flame—in anything, really.

Surveillance algorithms track us like this. For the first third of the movie, the creature surveys the team from its silent post, invisible. I think it's watching Dutch, but as we're also watching Dutch, it also turns to us: it's watching us watching it. That's the subtext of the film as seen these years later: through the Predator's eye we are revealed for what we are: animal and cruel. No better for our sonneteering and our musicals and our occasionally advanced consciousness of race. Good sci-fi works like this: through it we see ourselves anew.

It's a role reversal this late in the film. Finally Dutch is the one surveying Predator: we are in his POV, his body heat camouflaged by caked-on mud, the roles reversed. The man's set this trap for the alien. He'll shoot an arrow at it weakly in a moment. That's one of the weirdest shots in the film: though it's a homemade scavenged arrow and a homemade bow, which is definitely cool, still we watch the arrow twang unimpressively off-screen. It misses its target and the thing rears, alerted to the shift: now the Predator is prey, or at least it and Dutch are the hunter and the hunted equally.

I stare at that face I found in the swirling fire. You can't unsee a face once you notice it. Tell this to killers. Only they can know how their victims' faces follow them. Maybe it's a comfort to think it: that there is some retribution for our actions in the world. It's not as strong a cosmic move as being outmatched and eviscerated by an alien, but you can't have everything all the time.

FLASH FROM this nascent showdown to another: the last chapter of the graphic novel *Archie vs. Predator*, one panel in particular, after the teen Predator, kind of obsessed with Betty and Veronica (who isn't?), has wounded the titular Archie, probably mortally. The comic has already shown itself willing to kill off characters who never ever die in the original strand of the comics. Like in *Predator*, we're slowly winnowing out the characters until we get down to the final four: Betty, Veronica, Archie, and Jughead. Jughead gets decapitated by the teenage Predator, and then Archie next, and now we're down to the two girls, the central versus at the center of the Archie universe: Betty, the sweet blond, and Veronica, the conniving brunette.

I remember reading Archie comics at my grandma Ann's house on Pelican Lake in Minnesota. They were the only popular media I remember her having, and they had only been popular, it seemed like, twenty years before. I rummaged through the guest bedroom where I stayed in search of something to keep me occupied, and Archie comics were the best option I could find. Why did she even have them at all? I can't imagine her reading Archie comics, nor her kids, not really. They were the old ones: or, well, let's be honest, Archie always seemed old to me, an artifact of a bygone time, and that was the case for Archie up until the second decade in the twenty-first century, when all of a sudden—I don't know the story, but clearly some reins got passed to folks with a more open mind—those in control of the Archie empire loosened way the fuck up, with *Afterlife with Archie*, in which a zombie apocalypse comes to Riverdale, which could not have been more different than the Archie I remember from my grandma's cottage. I couldn't believe that people *ever* read this shit, I remember telling myself. And it's probably unfair, in retrospect: what did I know about the adult world I so craved then? It sure seemed dull, like what you imagine your grandma was always into must have been dull, even though the older you get the less obvious that conclusion seems. But I distinctly remember how reading those comics confirmed for me my belief that comics were beneath my interest, even as dorky as those interests were (my obsession with computer games was certainly no cooler).

I was surprised to come back to Archie, in part through *Afterlife with Archie*, and then *Archie vs. Predator*, and I've become enveloped in some of the television versions of the Archie universe, having watched all of the shows *Riverdale* and *The Chilling Adventures of Sabrina*. I hope some of my prejudice against Archie and the thing it's a synecdoche for, comics in general, has worn away. In a lot of ways, *Predator* was a comic to begin with, with everything big and caricatured, moving from setpiece—the attack on the guer-rilla camp!—to setpiece—the shooting blindly into the jungle!—to setpiece—the final showdown with the alien! So I don't know why I'm surprised by the greatness and ridiculousness of *Archie vs. Predator*, but it is great, and I love a lot about it, though the one panel that sticks with me is this:

The girls have (don't ask) activated a self-destruct mechanism in Veronica's house, and in the previous panel, Betty tells Veronica, "I'm not sure this is a good idea, Veronica," as they're dragging Archie to, we're told, some medical lab at the center of the man-sion where they're hoping Archie can be saved. (This is not much more batshit than *Predator* itself, honestly.) Then we get to the central panel on the page, in which Veronica says in response to Betty's questioning, "No. The bad idea was relying on boys to do things for us. . . . Boys never do anything right, Betty."

BACK IN THE FILM the Predator rears and responds to Dutch's homemade explosive arrow, however weakly it was shot, firing in the direction from which it senses the arrow came. When the shots hit something, sparks explode everywhere, illuminating the jungle. This repeats for quite a while.

The week of July 4th in America, we all know, is days of hid-ing pets and interrupted sleep, days of being reminded that we are among bombs and other instruments of war, days in which we're contingent and only survive on account of those who fight on our behalf, or days of being reoriented every few minutes to the sound of something exploding somewhere closer than it ought to be and the response of furious adolescent glee and a guilt chaser after.

If we sing the national anthem loud enough, no one we love will ever die.

Fires burn beyond the mountain. Fires burn on the mountain. I can see them at night from my backyard, an evil-looking line moving diagonally all the way up it. It looks like lava flow. It looks like apocalypse. I can see the tree of smoke and the cloud it feeds into as I hope for rain to help curb its spread. If I knew how it started, would it help my sleep? If I understood how a man could shoot a nine-year-old in a crowd, would it be easier to take myself apart and figure out what's wrong? If madmen (or anyone) were reducible, maybe we wouldn't have to quarantine them from the rest of us. It's not only punishment but fear that keeps them there and us out here: I am as capable as the rest of you of acts of extreme emotion and a lifetime of regret after.

An explosion lights my sky into a movie sky. It sets back the darkness only some as it lights and spreads. In the movie this would mean a battle between a man and an alien, but outside my window it means a holiday. All this noise and light might be an irritant now, but once it meant awe. Remember buying fireworks from the reservation, where everything was legal? It was you who bought all those cherry bombs and M-80s, right? You wanted to blow up mailboxes? Huge spools of telephone line? Trash cans? Small cars? It was you who was the agent of explosions then, I want to tell myself and my friends.

Just be careful, no one told you, and you were not. It wasn't the fireworks that changed you but the homemade bombs you built to try and nudge the needle on the world. Maybe it was to out-run or outweigh the racist remarks you threw at friends, the ass-holes you were then to each other, and, sure, you were good to each other, too, at times and in your ways. Other days you'd try to break each other down for our amusement. It was cold. There was no Predator. We had to stay inside for months. Our parents had whatever on their minds. At least we weren't on drugs (mostly) and dropping out of school (mostly).

I dunno: these stories seem overblown when seen from decades away. We all made it through scarred variously, unlikely to return. Some of us turned to drink or drugs or sex or violence or other thrills or love or something less. These are stories I gather up around me and wear underneath my clothes like an explosive vest. Probably it's not fucked: it's fine. Probably it was just a film. Probably everyone's okay except for the arrests and broken marriages and suicides and worse ways to die. There are few good ways, we understand, as more mount in combinations we had never imagined. Suicide by hanging off the side of a water tower. Overdosed. Institutionalized. A couple of DUIs, at least the ones I know about. Files kept on all of us by the FBI, the NSA, and other agencies built to keep tabs on those like us, those kids who blew shit up and espoused anarchist views. Or worse, to have not even gotten noticed or written up. For the world to have witnessed our shitty overtures and to remain unmoved.

Yet none of us continue to be threats, at least unless we're threatened.

But what's the use? How many actually move the world through our actions? It's a sucker's game anyway, my midwesternness replies: just try to be good, or, failing that, which we know you will, be okay, or, failing that, shut up about your pain already: we all hurt and burn in our own ways. We are no more or less individual than you. Let's all pipe down and watch the stars explode on whichever sky or screen you like and be moved.

DUTCH GETS WINGED by one of the Predator's shots. His lip is cut. On account of the explosions, the Predator's camouflaging cloak no longer works. I notice now how Schwarzenegger's beautiful spiked hair is slimed with mud. He chucks another explosive spear. It seems to have injured the Predator: we see bits of the creature's blood—a luminescent green—splattered on a rock. Is it a trap? Of course it is. It has to be.

Dutch follows the trail of blood into the darkness—a cave, I guess. It's blood that's led him here, Paul Monette doesn't have to tell me. It drips behind him from the ceiling. How's it on the ceiling? Something's wrong. Then he knows he's trapped. The creature's got him now. But then he sets off a flash grenade and runs. The thing blasts its gun behind him. He falls into a pool, tracers of light following him from an explosion.

His mud sheath's now gone, and so the thing has finally found him here. It pins his neck with a pair of blades. I mean BLADES. It could kill Dutch in this moment. But instead it lifts him up as if he were a toy and throws him against a tree. Confident again in its superiority it pauses and takes stock of him face-to-face. In this shot we also see how much bigger the creature is than Schwarzenegger: at least a foot. And here's the shot of how Dutch's face looks in the creature's heat-light POV: like a radiant skull, a black hole for a nose, contours of blues and greens and yellows and reds, dashes of purple and even a little white for the hottest part of the eyes. Holding Dutch, the Predator turns his face back and forth as if in appraisal. What is this beautiful, dirty thing it has been fighting all this time?

This scene isn't in the novelization or the script before they started shooting, so it's an invention during filming, and it's a great one: here we get to see what we've been wanting to see the whole movie: what the very best of us—Dutch—looks like to the thing from space. Here we see again what we look like from a perspective other than our own. It's an opportunity we're offered. Will we take it? What will we make of it?

Let's pause the film here and hold this shot, if only for a minute. I set this scene—thirteen seconds, punctuated by a brief shot of the Predator face-to-face with Dutch—to loop. This self-seeing is the story of the movie. So much of what we've seen—all this destruction, all these explosions, all these beautiful bloody sequences of guns and shooting and violence and men and men and men on men—it's all been from the team's POV. The American POV. The male POV. We're the ones here under false pretenses, illegally operating in another country, armed to the teeth and ready to fire and fire and fire and keep firing on whatever until we're exhausted. Why? The movie's wise not to push the point too hard: no one wants a thesis balanced in the bullets. These are characters, not only the objects of ideas, which is what makes the movie work, but that doesn't mean it's *just* action we've been watching. It can be action and it can be terror and it can be a growing sense of un-ease we should be feeling with our own tendencies and behaviors, what we didn't know we learned, or maybe I'm only talking about myself here, what I didn't know I learned watching this movie so many times and being permeable to it. I mean, let's let ourselves look, just look, and feel, just feel, at least for this moment between explosions.

AND LIKE THAT the Predator lets him go. For some reason it lets him go. It releases him, not ungently. The moment's over. It steps away. Starts to disconnect its mask. Now it wants Dutch to see its face, or perhaps it wants to see its foe unfiltered.

It's an elaborate process, disrobing in front of another man. One has a lot of gear. Tubes get disconnected. Straps come off. Armor is discarded. We hear it hit the ground. There is the sound of pneumatic tubes. Finally the mask is off and we see it as it is: insect-like, or maybe reptilian, with four mandibles that click. There's a hint of vagina dentata to the thing, and it's no surprise that horror comes from here. Schwarzenegger gets another of his famous lines: "You're one ugly motherfucker." I'm not even sure which word to italicize in that line for emphasis. It's delivered so well. It gets delivered in a maximally Schwarzeneggerian accent: "You're one. Ugly. Motherfucker." It's funny because it's true, but sure, it hurts to hear.

The thing responds with clicks, as if it acknowledges the fact, then it gives a roar befitting an apex predator. It flexes then moves closer. We can see in its POV that its vision is much less sensitive now that the mask's come off: everything now is shades of red.

〈28〉

Lament for the Man inside the Suit

YOU DIDN'T NEED THERMAL VISION there in Mexico on location to know it wasn't cold—hot as a hole that led to hell—and eight times worse inside the suit. Few humans will ever get to know its weight or what it means to don the mask and represent our ways. No one thought to ask me how hard it is to move in it (I would have liked a credit in the film) and what the meat is like underneath. You believed I was just a story, but stories come from somewhere.

Kevin Peter Hall (1955–1991), you know now how playing monsters monsters you. They say it's only a role and not a hole you shoot through and become some double—not it not you but else, the two at once, a thaumatrope, what they called a motion picture the last time I visited this planet. It was another age: steam and stink and every cage filled with bird; every gallows held a noose: nothing was without its other. Death was omnipresent then. Now you hide your old and frail away in homes and hope to be away on vacay so as to miss their ends.

You don't bury or burn your own—instead, they're sent out to be embalmed in basement labs. The casket costs a fortune, to say

nothing of the chemicals, the headstone, and the plot. You believe you can outthink disease. That a surgery will save you. That
your behavior changes because you tweet. Civilization does not
become you. Still, you play a role and begin to understand the other
creature, at least a little.

I've worn a suit of human skin to see if I could pass. Not superwell, though I was beautiful, I thought, in it, in you, dressed up in
your species's shame in the changing room at H&M after it had
closed, enough illumination from the security lights so I could
turn and see myself in infrared, a ballerina inside an oyster shell.
I swear I glistened there.

For a moment I admit I was bewitched; I could maybe even have
been in love, though on a second look the seams did show. Your
skin's so soft, I thought, until it dries. What made you hard inside?
You did get hard. You had to be to live this way, contained (so they
believed) in the cliché *gentle giant*. What if instead you'd rioted and
burned the set with size, put the leading actors in their place, made
the close-up yours and never let it go?

If you hadn't contracted HIV from a blood transfusion and
died from complications, we could have fought without our second skins, and flowered into something else. We had an opening
but didn't take it. Now I don't—I can't, I think—have friends. We
are too strong, you see. We belong alone. From the way you moved
after the take was done I believe you knew this too.

In the end there's only you, the camera, light, your need for
blood, the jungle heat, the suit, the victor's call, the loser's wail, the
simplicity of violence. It becomes a history. No great mystery: be
the silencer or learn to live in silence.

29

What in the Hell Are You?

LET'S LOOK AT THE THING A LITTLE LONGER. The creature's beautiful in its own way, credibly alien, but humanoid. Here's where all the money spent on the special effects pays off.

Looking in my Predator folder for the script to compare this scene against I stumble on a file I downloaded four years ago on David Allen Goodreau, the "budding serial killer and presumed serial rapist" who murdered my childhood friend Chris's sister Jodi and Kathryn Nankervis, another young woman whose name I hadn't heard before. When working on an earlier draft of this book I had found some material on him while looking up information on the murder trial. I remembered aspects of the story, though the fact of it—having someone I knew, someone who'd babysat me when she was younger, and an older sister of my friend, murdered—clearly had affected me deeply. I didn't follow the case, though I remained friends with her brother throughout, if at an increasing distance, as my family moved to Saudi Arabia.

The file I saved describes Goodreau in inexcusably lurid (and frankly lazy) ways: "He never drank or smoked. He raised two delightful children and faithfully attended church. He had a job that helped others, and he had amiable chats with neighbors. But David Allen Goodreau had everybody fooled—he was a killer; he would secretly kill and then kill again. . . . mild-mannered and unassuming . . . he hardly looked or even acted like a serial rapist or killer. A spiritual man . . ." and so on.

I had forgotten his name, along with many of the details of the event, though listening to a true crime podcast on the events reminded me. I'm glad I don't remember his name. One shouldn't. These predators—it's hard to use any other word—should not merit our attention or the fame we accord them. It's easy to understand why they fascinate, aberrant as they are. They suggest we are all capable of what they do. At least in some moments we are, I suppose, but there's plenty that holds us back. What held back Goodreau was not enough. His family didn't hold him back. His mild-manneredness didn't hold him back. His milquetoast government job didn't hold him back. His devoutness didn't hold him back. The *Ironwood Daily Globe* reported in 1994 some details of his confession, that "satanic forces" drove him to kill the women. There's lurid for you, and who knows, maybe it's true. Many of us like to look at terrible people. We're fascinated by them. We look and look and look. When I see Schwarzenegger looking at the Predator, and the Predator looking at Schwarzenegger, I see myself looking at a killer—Goodreau, sure, but also Loughner.

Seeing Goodreau described in exactly these ways reminds me a lot—at the risk of spoiling a nice plot twist—of *Predators*, the third stand-alone in the *Predator* franchise (I'm not counting the *AvP* movies, as they exist somewhat separately). It's a good movie and totally worth the watch, a nice throwback to and development of the world of *Predator*, in which a bunch of super-hard-core earthlings (not only Americans and not only guys, finally) are abducted and put on an alien planet that functions as a game preserve . . . for predators. The creatures come to hunt them, our heroes fight back and mostly die, etc., but it turns out that the one harmless-seeming guy, played by Topher Grace, is actually among the most dangerous of them. We learn this mild-mannered dork of a man is a serial killer toward the end. He could almost be patterned after Goodreau.

In LA's exceptionally tabloidy and at-least-a-little-nauseating Museum of Death, there are rooms devoted to murders and others to serial killers, including signed letters from some of them. Crime scene photos and murder and stalking memorabilia are all over. It can be a rough ride, since it offers no contemporary framework through which to see or think about these things except to say, hey, check this crazy shit out. It's disturbing because it conflates all kinds of strangenesses in one space. Here are lurid crime scene photographs from a fucked-up Detroit murder spree next to a sorta anthropological exhibit about nineteenth-century funeral practices, next to some probably fake shrunken heads and then a 1990s-era video about closeted gay Hollywood icons and a room about celebrity stalkers and what is only probably a reproduction of a bedroom from the Heaven's Gate compound (it could be real). No attempt appears to have been made to think how these things are related, or how fucked up they are and in what ratio, and who ought to be complicit in presenting or looking at any of these things. A neon sign outside the museum reads, "Death is everywhere."

I was working on a book about archives and libraries, and found myself at the Kinsey Sex Research Institute's archive at Indiana University, and I remember one of the archivists showing me some of the weirder stuff they had in their collections. I mean, it's a sex archive, after all, so weird is the name of the game. It's also a serious archive, open only to those with an academic affiliation, and the archivists clearly mean to present everything with the utmost discretion, but it's also silly, as much of our sexual lives are, frankly, when viewed from outside the bubble of our desires.

There's a ton of amateur and professional erotica and surely plenty of material that the government has deemed obscene. I looked at the private sex diaries of couples, including explicit photographs they'd taken throughout their lives. You want dildos? A nineteenth-century bibliography of works about flagellation? Corset fetish scrapbooks? Magazine features on 1940s female impersonators in Flint, Michigan? I mean they have almost anything in the range of human sexuality. I saw only a sliver of their holdings. But they also have at least one painting of a clown by serial killer John Wayne Gacy that they showed me almost as an afterthought. I don't remember why they had it exactly except that it was part of a bequest they had received, and they didn't know what to do with it, as the archivist told me. They certainly weren't going to exhibit it. You can't sell it—ethically, she said. It's tempting to burn it, but it is part of the archive after all. Start burning things and where do you stop? At any rate, it's burned now in my memory—the image of it, the experience of being presented with it in person.

I went back into my archives from that trip and found I hadn't taken a photo of the painting itself, or perhaps I'd deleted it since, not wanting to reproduce it, but I had documented the fact of it: its packaging and the signature attached. It's 10" x 14", on a "Fredrix Quality Artist Canvas Panel." Titled *Skull Clown*, it's signed by Gacy and with a note attached: "Enjoy this painting as much as I enjoyed doing it for you. Best wishes, John W Gacy." I'm sure if you do some googling you can find one of his images to give you the idea, but I'd encourage you not to do so if you can stop yourself.

In my trip archives these documents are between a set of nineteenth-century female nudes (as dirty as any pornography you can imagine: let us not believe in 2021 we have a monopoly on filth) they had displayed in one of their galleries and a 1974 ASCII art nudie calendar printed out with a dot matrix printer with the tear-away printer. It features a woman with improbably large breasts, as rendered in the letters A, I, C, V, and X (mostly X), among others. Xs and Os comprise her nipples. They use P, U, S, S, and Y to shade her pubic hair.

I mean, this is what I'm looking at, in part, when I'm looking at the alien: I'm watching a digital file of an analog movie in which special effects and makeup are representing an alien life-form, something truly unknowable, except we do get to be inside it as it regards us, also similarly unknowable. I mean, really I'm watching it and remembering myself watching it and trying to overlay all these experiences on top of one another and also enjoy the thing it does to me. It's a weird and memorable headfuck of an experience. I mean, I'm looking at the other thing, the thing beyond comprehension, except here it is in front of us—in front of Dutch. I'm looking at it, and it's looking at Schwarzenegger, and I'm looking at Schwarzenegger like it's looking at Schwarzenegger, and in fact I'm looking at us, aren't I, some of our very worst parts—the violence and the mania for guns, the homophobia, the racism, the wanton disregard for human rights or ethics, generally—but also some of our best: ingenuity, a sense of decency, resilience, friendship and camaraderie, curiosity, our ability to make a joke of almost anything, our honor. Even beauty is what I'm looking at, both in the way the film is shot and, of course, in Schwarzenegger's face, and his incredibly well-sculpted biceps and abs. I'm looking at our ability to rape and murder and fuck with native populations for reasons we tell ourselves are maybe good going in, and all the collateral damage it creates for generations, and I'm looking at the way what seems to be an action movie is interested in looking at masculinity in maybe a little different way than we imagined going in.

I am looking at the victims of all of this, too, even if the movie doesn't want me to. There are so many. At least eighty-six characters die on-screen in *Predator*, primarily guerrillas. The odd thing is that after the big shootout in the camp, actually, very few die. Only eight—including the Predator—in the last seventy-five minutes of the film.

Before Goodreau, you'd have to go back a century to find the most recent murder in my hometown. And yet no one connected the two murders—both of young, petite women—for more than eighteen months. The first death, that of Kathy Nankervis, was barely covered. I don't even remember hearing about it, and I lived there! For some context, the town had approximately 6,000 residents, and another 3,500 students at Michigan Tech University. Watts's death sent a shock wave through the town, certainly. People started locking their doors. The MTU campus police force was allowed, for the first time ever, to carry guns. We all knew that death was present in this place, however. Many had died in the mines. A neighbor blew his face off with a gun, but failed to kill himself, then later completed the job. We all knew stories of people who died in the snow, who went through thin ice on a snowmobile, for example. I remember a neighbor electrocuted himself on his roof and fell and died. Relatives died of emphysema or heart attacks. My mother died of cancer.

It was only after another woman called 911 on hearing someone try to break into her house that the police finally apprehended Goodreau. He was outside her home wearing latex gloves and carrying a bag that held duct tape, a pry bar, and a video camera, among other items. He admitted he was planning on breaking in, and later admitted to killing the other two women. The true crime podcasts call his bag "a kill bag," a term in common parlance on those shows, and its ubiquity tells you plenty about the way they (by which I mean we) fetishize these stories.

WHEN I'M LOOKING at the Predator, though, I'm also seeing something that has a code of honor, as we've come to understand. It may be alien but it will not attack the unarmed or weak or small. When Dutch calls it "one ugly motherfucker," is it the *thing* that's truly ugly? Really? And what does *ugly* here mean anyway? It means *unlike us*, which in many contexts could be as much of a compliment as an insult.

Anyway, I'm not going to give you the play-by-play for the ensuing fight between them because it's all a little bit dumb, especially when narrated, because this is where we get back to *Rocky vs. E.T.* It's in these set pieces that the film returns to its action movie sensibility.

Instead, let's focus on the strange moments in the film on either side of the predictable ones. Let's pause the action to go frame by frame for a moment. At 1:36:42 we see, in the Predator's POV, Dutch, we assume, in the infrared, as a blur, as he tries to attack the thing, maybe with a piece of wood? I'm not sure. As it's a blur, when I move frame by frame I can't tell at all what's happening: here's some red and pink and maybe a little black and blue. It's an abstract image, looked at alone. There are a lot of them. But when chained, in a moment we see an outstretched hand appear—Dutch's again. It's almost as if he is reaching out to us, the viewers (if you're still with me, then we remain a we, though I'm willing to accept it may just be me at this point), and pressing his hand on the screen. It's only there for a fraction of a second, enough to notice it, but not to fascinate on it, and then it's gone, resolved into the Predator's hand/claw thing adorned by a cool computer panel that will come to mean more in a few minutes. I know this isn't the way the movie's made to be seen, but it's how it's made, and when I can still a thing I can reduce it to its component parts. I can think about it and see how beautiful it is and how many mysteries it contains. That these mysteries are perhaps ones that I alone can see only deepens them.

The world is filled with mysteries. Some resolve, some don't. When you're young the world is made of mysteries. It's a gift, I recognize, to see the world this way, and not to have, like most adults, a sense that you generally know what it's all about. That things are settled, solved. This is a gift the Predator gives these guys—especially Dutch, who gets to see the most of it—before it kills them. Our world is not what we thought it was. We are not alone, for instance. We are not the apex predators, as we once believed. We believe in mastery—it's more comfortable to believe this way—but we ought to believe in mystery instead.

When a few years back scientists finally solved one of my

Michigan's outstanding mysteries, the Paulding Light, I was saddened. It is a poorer world with what seemed like an unanswerable and beguiling question solved. That must be part of the appeal of the serial killer, how the aberration suggests the mystery of the human mind and its many hidden drives: he is us but he is alien.

I COULD WATCH these Predator POV scenes forever. They are rich beyond compare. They're the secret to the movie's greatness. Since we don't quite know what we're seeing when we're seeing them, we are presented with our own limitations, and it feels at times legitimately alien. Not so alien as to be beyond comprehension (one might imagine what the Xenomorph in the movie *Alien* sees, should we get its POV, would be too intense and fractured to even bear). But this Predator, he's enough like us. He is a *he*, for instance. That much is clear. He acts like a he. Maybe a better he than our men are. These scenes are almost the most abstract, and hold me the longest because they hold the most mystery. They are the least like the action movie grammar I've become so comfortable within.

It pains me to unpause these POV scenes and to return to the more predictable world of the big showdown at the end. This is the climax of the film, as we all know, and is structurally required. But the action/outcome is far less interesting than these internecine moments and the spaces they create. Here's Dutch getting his ass kicked. Here's a ribbon of blood spraying out of his mouth. More and more blood. We see it again—I think: I can't quite tell—in infrared from a couple of angles, for effect, like the memorable triple slow-motion punch replay from *Rocky IV*. This is the moment in the movie where the movie really lives up to the joke that gave birth to it: here, after all the rest of what we've been through together, we finally have *Rocky vs. E.T.*

That this is in the alien's POV makes it more effective. The close-ups of Dutch's face in infrared also negate his great personal beauty, even beaten as he is. And beaten-up he is. The Predator is master now. Dutch crawls slowly away, injured and exhausted, followed by the Predator. He desperately drags himself to a crack in the rocks. We see this is his trap: he wants the thing to come in to kill him. He yells at it: "Come on! Do it! Do it! Come on! Come on! Kill me! I'm here! Kill me! I'm here! Kill me! Come on! Kill me! I'm here! Come on! Do it now! Kill me!"

But it does not. Sensing, perhaps, the obvious trap, or perhaps because it is familiar enough with us not to always take what men say at face value, it does not enter the crack but moves around the side. But Dutch has one more trap to spring, so he does, kicking out a stick that triggers a log that falls on the creature, finally crushing it.

A shot of Dutch's face, finally drained of tension—for a moment. Then we see the log rising, the creature struggling to lift it. Dutch snaps to, picks up a rock and stands with it over the alien as if to crush it. His grimace tells us he is the animal now. Is there honor in finishing the thing this way? The alien is spitting up green luminescent blood.

This green luminescent blood—such a cool effect—turns out to be exactly what it looks like: activated glow sticks, broken open. We learn this from the director's commentary, in which he describes how they tried, like, thirty kinds of liquids and pastes and creams, and eventually someone figured out you could break a glow stick, so low tech, and it worked fantastically.

I can't believe I'd never broken one until a couple years ago. Every Saturday night the tradition in our house is that my daughter gets a glow stick. We bought a ton of them from the dollar store. I love their cheap effect, how beautiful they look in the dark, how when spun or whipped around during a bedtime conversation in a dark room, for instance, their light trails look almost solid because our eyesight isn't quite quick enough to track their motion. The effect is nothing short of magic, and my daughter loves them, and they're cheap, so she gets them every week because why not? I like to play with them, too, though usually I'll sneak in after she's asleep and place my lit glow stick on her pillow so she has two. One night I was whipping one around in the living room, my daughter not quite yet sleeping, my wife not particularly amused with my cool whipping skills, and the glow stick broke and splashed luminescent goo all over my face and arm and the couch and wall. Just how evil *was* this shit? I wondered. Like, did I need to wash it off immediately? Surely it couldn't be poisonous: We couldn't be *that* dumb, could we? I liked the look of it striped across my face, even as I was surprised, how dramatically the scene had changed with the application of this glowing chemical concoction, so I yelled, and my daughter came out of her room to look at this crazy thing that had happened, and when she was looking at her dad's face glowing green and laughing hilariously, she cut her foot—quite badly—on the plastic edge of the treadmill, which we didn't notice at the time, and only figured out when she came out a minute later covered in blood, obviously shocked at the fact of it all over her, and so my wife and I had to take her to the urgent care a few miles away. She was, of course, superpissed about getting cut, about having to go somewhere in the middle of the night, and she was flipping out. She shrieked all the way to urgent care in the car: "Kill Me! Just Kill Me! Kill me now! I don't want to live!" It was hard not to laugh as we tried to get her to the choppa where she would get her stitches and her scar.

ON-SCREEN THERE IS BLOOD, all glowing green. At least we know it's not ours. Very badly injured and covered in its wet insides, suddenly outside of it—surely among the most terrible feelings—the creature coughs. More glowing green comes up. Poised to crush it, Dutch softens. So instead of killing it with the rock, he drops it onto what looks like a pile of ashes on the jungle floor. And we get the final classic moment of the movie. He asks the dying Predator, "What the hell *are* you?" And it responds, after a moment, repeating what he said, like it had before, with a little different emphasis, just enough to shift our attention: "What the hell are *you*?"

Both versions of the script and the novelization offer something different, in which Dutch asks not *what* but *who* the hell are you? The movie's shifting the *who* to *what* makes it not about Dutch but about our natures and seeing them.

The script goes on to tell us that "Schaefer's body looms over him, MOTTLED and STREAKED from his exposed skin, blood oozing from his shoulder wound, his eyes like black sockets in his almost skull-like face. Seen from this perspective, Schaefer is a frightening, horrible visage." Which—again—yes. Who's the ugly motherfucker now?

The whole confrontation with the alien takes much longer in the movie than in the versions of the scripts I'm reading, in which it only takes up a couple of pages. The scripts don't have the alien taking off its mask, or their maskless hot-man-on-thing fight, or the many moments in which the thing is kicking Schwarzenegger's ass. In the scripts, the movie's conclusion comes in different ways than the one we're watching happen. I imagine they rewrote it as they remade the choreography in filming and as McTiernan realized both the opportunities the story presented as well as the limitations of the budget.

In the script Dutch acquires the Predator's weapon and pursues the injured thing through the forest, ending the chase into the alien's spacecraft where he kills the alien as it takes off, and the ship explodes, nearly killing Dutch too. This would be both very expensive to film and dumb: some mysteries we don't need resolved. How much of the alien's mythology do we really need to know right now?

Back in the film, instead, presumably dying, the Predator opens up its alien arm console thing, clicks some alien console stuff, and begins what it takes Dutch a bit to figure out is a countdown. And it laughs—or it reproduces and repurposes Billy's remarkable laughter from earlier as he finally got the last of Hawkins's jokes. It's Billy's laugh, but amplified and distorted, almost as if to say, I'm gonna have me some FUN tonight.

The laughter becomes more and more insane and desperate—another repetition to exhaustion—as it goes on, and Dutch runs as the Predator's ALIEN ARM CONSOLE counts down and then the whole scene explodes in a mushroom CLOUD, presumably the effect of some kind of tactical nuke. It isn't the best effect, and the movie knows it, cutting quickly to smoke and more smoke.

In fact, the whole scene now is smoke, and through it we see the CHOPPA arriving, with Anna (who did, in fact, get to the choppa) and the GENERAL and a couple of helicopter pilots, one played by Kevin Peter Hall in a cameo role, so we finally see the face of the man who donned the Predator suit for the whole film, which must have been brutal work.

And amidst the SMOKE and all the burning and destroyed THINGS is a shirtless, shell-shocked Dutch amidst a huge pile of burned-down and still-aflame jungle.

This shot is scored by a single trumpet in what at first sounded to me like a near riff on "Taps" suggesting both lament for all those who were lost (at least the Americans) and victory, if a narrow one, for Dutch, America, and by extension humanity, or as the movie probably imagines it, "man," meaning not only the general term for humans but men specifically. Men did this. Men did *all* of this.

The novel tells us "It was Schaefer, but looking for all the world as if *he* were the alien."

It's not "Taps," though, that it's referencing, at least not directly. McTiernan tells us in the director's commentary that "we used some Aaron Copland—I've since learned the name of the piece is 'Fanfare for the Common Man.' [Film composer Alan] Silvestri later parodied it beautifully—we called it 'Fanfare for the Common Mercenary.'"

The script describes Anna and Dutch exchanging "a faint smile," but there is no smile in the film. We're left with its opposite: we see a close-up of the face of a completely wrecked (but of course still beautiful) Dutch, bloodied and covered in mud, not looking at anything really. In fact, he's clearly looking at nothing, like they were shooting at nothing. He's not even looking. His eyes are open but they're not looking. What does *looking* even mean? He's seen enough. He's done enough. I hope we've seen enough. We zoom in on his face. His eyes move finally, after a few seconds, toward the open choppa window and the forest underneath.

The novel tells us, "As he stared at the sky hints of pink and gold splashed across the Conta Mana border, announcing the coming of day."

Or as the script puts it, "Pull away and head towards the distant, green horizon. FADE OUT."

30

Lament for the Men inside the Suits

LAMENT NOT JUST FOR YOU, Kevin Peter Hall, the body inside the body on the screen, but you too, Monette, whom I never met except in these sentences that gave voice to not only an alien but all the men inside. What might it mean for us to meet like this? In a Safeway, say?

I wonder: How many men did you meet in a safe way? What is a safe way to meet men or anyone? Your last journal lists sixteen of them: Doug (5'8", 140), Paul (hairy, cut, works out), Pete (Australian, medical, hot tub), Dave (876-xxxx), Rick (850-xxxx), Tom (662-xxxx), Joe (2 AM, 5'10", gymnast wrestler blond, Virginian / Iowa / talk dirty), Bob (33, full leather), Doug (23, 5'10", brown, 145), Lorenzo (669-xxxx), Chris (2 AM weekends), Bill (late afternoon, 784-xxxx), Gary (Indianapolis, 5'10" hairy, works out), Mark (smooth, Hawaiian, v. evolved), Joe (NY Italian, hairy, mustache, runs a club), Rob (the lost connection, clothespins). (I edited out the really dirty parts to safekeep some things.)

I go to the Safeway every year, the place where Giffords was meeting constituents, some men some not, or where she had set up shop to hear them anyway, the voices of those she was trying to represent in Congress, the Safeway where she was shot, where those others were, where good guys with guns failed to protect us from a bad guy with a gun. She would have thought it safe, that corner. It's as safe as any way these days (which is to say not safe at all: we are not safe in any way). I bought some things: a new flavor of Cheerios. An avocado. Flowers for the memorial. Six or seven beers. Five died there, in the corner of this Safeway in my city: Tucson, Arizona. Christina Taylor-Green, nine, dead on arrival at the hospital. I left a copy of *Love Alone* at the memorial.

Monette and Hall: you both died nearly thirty years ago. I can still see you both on-screen. I can see it all on-screen. I watched it all on-screen, the news, my face facing it as news came in that Giffords had been shot, had died. In the hour to come that was revised: she was alive, in critical condition. They had subdued the shooter; he was in custody. His photograph. His name.

Now both of you are dead, oddly both of complications related to HIV. Gifford lives, if a somewhat rerouted life. Her husband recently won a Senate seat as I edited this manuscript, in part on a platform of sensible gun control. I remain hopeful. Loughner and Goodreau live, too, though diminished, or at least thankfully contained. It is unknown to what degree they are haunted or aware. It is unknown to what degree they were impregnated by aliens in action films. I am alive: I believe undiminished but who's to say. Is it cowardice or kindness to imagine the diminished are the last to know?

I call to you who wore the suit before. I put mine on.

I call to you in the Predatorium: though we may hunt alone let us hunt together. Let us weed out the worst of us together.

Men: we are after becoming. It's our way of opening men and then becoming them. What are we after we have become? I wonder. What makes us men? Is it the safety we project or the terror we inflect? Monette: you'd tell me the only way you can become a man is to know one from the inside. Predator agrees, though with different methodologies. Since it can't assume our form it wants to know what we contain, as if we are what we contain. (Are we what we contain?) All art affects what it depicts, though we don't like to admit it. As if we could even know the ether or the jar, being one with both.

What if we were no more than collections of echoes? Of our fathers' lists or our mothers' self-regard (or the reverse)? Of all the corporal punishments. Of all our errors. Of the things we did and that were done to us? What we wanted done to us? Some of these things we thought or watched but didn't do were terrible: all of us, our terrible. You and I, our terrible together. What did we do that brought terror and to whom? What if we're the echoes of the force we projected into the world?

All I ask is for us to see ourselves: to look and also to see. To know what we can be and what we can do.

"If it bleeds, we can kill it," Schwarzenegger says. Meaning that if we can diminish it then we can finish it. I know it is a diminishment I offer you, this calling up your evanescence, this naming from the grave.

Let's start by drawing blood. When it bleeds, we'll know we can kill it.

I have thought of killing thee, Loughner and Goodreau, in whatever form and contained in whatever detention camp they have you in. I have fantasized—even before I knew you—even before you were born—about how would I break into a place like this, which guard I would disable first, which weapon caches I would set to blow. How my raid on the detention camp could play out like *Predator* or like how I learn in games I love that these scenarios are fun puzzles for us to solve. When I do all the assassin side quests in the Elder Scrolls games I am preparing myself for you.

All of us are puzzles in need of solving. Monette gave us the most with his work, which we call a body of. That's enough of other for my ether. Hall, you were more a cipher: when on-screen you were almost always suited except in the helicopter at the end where you appear, uncredited, as a marine. All we have of you is the suits you wore and how you played the monsters and your grin, obvious in every interview: what luck it was to make a life of this!

Loughner and Goodreau, I don't want to wear your monsters. I'd rather that you wither in the dark.

How about we try something else instead?

There's an outtake from *Predator 2* (you can see it on YouTube) in which a whole group of Predators perform a coordinated dance. It's awesome, blossom, to watch them go, like *Solid Gold*, like *This Spartan Life*. Most of the guys they hired to play the other Predators were NBA players, LA Lakers, friends of Danny Glover, the sequel's star, and they came down to shoot some scenes as Predators. All geared up and terrifying as they were, I love that what they did was not to hunt and kill and look all menacing but to perform a kind of dorky dance together. All tools can be used in at least a couple of ways. It's up to us to find the ones that make new possibilities.

31

Curtain Call

ALL THINGS END, even novelizations, even novels, even books about dumb movies, and even people. Even Paul Monette. Even Jesse Ventura. Even Kevin Peter Hall. Even Sonny Landham. Even John McTiernan. Even Arnold Schwarzenegger. Even movies. Even *Predator.*

But as this one ends, *Predator* brings back our heroes for a curtain call at the beginning of the credits. One by one, all the major characters get to face the camera and get to crack a smile at last. Their characters may be dead, but the actors, it's important to know, are fine—or at least they were at the time. This is here to show that they had a good time. I like curtain calls like this. Even Ventura cracks a smile—almost. Only Bill Duke (Mac) and Schwarzenegger do not. Why not, I wonder?

In his curtain call, Hawkins is reading issue 408 of *Sgt. Rock*, a comic I've never read, after which the movie's characters were apparently closely modeled. The reference opens up another secret structure of the film. It's hard to know how much this particular issue means, but I can freeze the frame and zoom in. A close-up of the cover shows one geeky young soldier showing a beefy Sgt.

Rock a drawing he had made, saying, "I—I drew what war is REALLY like, Rock!" Rock looks grimly at the drawing, which we cannot see. Behind him we can see what looks like a transport with a backward swastika and a tank with a hole blown in the side of its turret. Text on the cover tells us, "This issue is dedicated to editor, artist, writer Shelly Mayer, creator of 'Scribbly' and 'Sugar and Spike,' and the catalyst for many of the people who are in comics today." It's not hard to imagine this is intentional, Shane Black (or maybe McTiernan or someone else) slyly referencing not only the comic, but this issue of the comic, dedicated to yet another artist, so the references stack.

McTiernan tells us he stole this curtain call bit from Robert Altman. He tells us he wanted "a 1950s kind of thing; we wanted to give them a curtain call, because the movie was a giant downer. We wanted to give the sense that we all had a good time making this: I hope you all had a good time watching it." And that is important. We had us some fun tonight, didn't we? *Predator* wears its brutality lightly. And as McTiernan says about the movie:

> It wasn't an instant overwhelming success or anything, like it didn't take the opening weekend or anything, but it's nice that it's been remembered since even it wasn't at the time a *sensation* or anything like that. It's got some nice stuff in it. Some stuff I like. It has a wonderful sort of childish suspension of disbelief that just goes for it. That's a lot of fun. I like that. I see the difference in the tone of the writing and the film-making in the early stuff and the later stuff. Personally I like the later stuff. It would have been nice to have been able to do the early stuff that way, but what the hell. It was only because I got through the early stuff well enough that I got a chance to make the rest of it.

I don't think we can just disavow the earlier stuff, the things we consumed and loved when we were young, before we became who we ended up being. I have no interest in disavowing *Predator* anyway. By now this should be obvious. I also wouldn't walk away from Stallone's *Cobra*, which I recently rewatched: it's not good, but it has flashes of weird excellence. *Red Heat* was a lot better than I remembered, and is worth revisiting for the incredible homoeroticism of the first couple of minutes of the movie, in which Arnold and a bunch of other dudes walk around, nearly nude, evidently in some kind of Russian bath or something, and then they fight nearly nude in the snow because of reasons. *Raw Deal* remains pretty bad. The sci-fi stuff holds up well: *Total Recall* continues to rule, as does *The Running Man*, in part because both were trying to tell us something about the future, and when that future came, they weren't far off. I watched *The Running Man* a couple of years ago, in the aftereffects of 2016's election. The movie starts with the following preamble:

> By 2017 the world economy has collapsed. Food, natural resources, and oil are in short supply. A police state, divided into paramilitary zones, rules with an iron hand. Television is controlled by the state and a sadistic game show called *The Running Man* has become the most popular program in history.

This didn't seem all that far off in 2017, and in the pandemic it seems even less far off. *Conan the Destroyer* is still okay. *Conan the Barbarian* remains excellent. *Red Sonja* was never good and still is bad but sure has a lot of budget for candles. *Twins* is better than you'd expect, as is *Kindergarten Cop*. *Terminator 2* (1991's top film) is excellent. *Last Action Hero* was meta then and is meta now and thus not all that good, and *True Lies*, *Eraser*, *End of Days*, and *The 6th Day* all start to move out of the sweet spot that was the late '80s and early '90s, and all of a sudden the era of these movies ended. Hair metal gave way to grunge.

Our anxieties turned extraterrestrial and scientific. The kind of action film *Predator* is no longer seemed as relevant. *Jurassic Park* certainly changed the blockbuster game in 1993. And even if *True Lies* still did well in 1994 (it still cracked the top 10), we don't remember it nearly as well as all those cloned dinos. Espionage films like the James Bond jams and *Mission: Impossible*s began moving up the charts; the superheroes started their ascension *(Batman Forever* cracked the top 10 in 1995), and disaster films made their mark *(Twister* in 1996, then *Deep Impact* in 1998). Aliens invaded and kept invading in 1996's *Independence Day,* and the world needed saving in new and different ways from *Godzilla* (1998) and meteors *(Armageddon* in 1997), and then the *Predator*s of the world were suddenly pretty much gone.

Men like these remained, however, and we grew up to be mostly unlike the kind of men we believed these men to be.

My mother died in 1982.

Roger Horwitz died in 1986. Monette's *Predator* is dedicated to him: "Achilles was not such a warrior / nor so mourned by his comrade-in-arms."

Kevin Peter Hall died in 1991.

Jodi Watts died in 1992.

Paul Monette died in 1995. According to his journal, here's what he proposed should be carved on his headstone: "Paul Monette / 1945–199_ / Lies Here at Last."

What is actually on his grave—not a headstone but a marker in the ground—is:

PAUL MONETTE
1945–1995
CHAMPION OF HIS PEOPLE
Here lie the remains
of a gentle loving poet
a valiant standardbearer
of liberty and humanity and compassion
Who arose from the pit of self-hatred
to proclaim his earthly rites

and blossom forth an exemplar
of great manly love
ΓΝΩΘΙ ΣΕΑΥΤΟΝ
"Remember, love will see us through."

The Greek translates to "Know thyself." I think this line from *Love Alone* (though it may well also have appeared in *Predator*) might have also fit: "What is written here is only one man's passing and one man's cry, a warrior burying a warrior."

Sonny Landham died in 2017.

As of this writing I am still alive.

END CREDITS

First, thanks to those who made *Predator*, whom, if you don't know their names by now, what book were you reading anyhow? But, since this is the credits, let's give credit where it's due. First to the some of the principals: John McTiernan, John and Jim Thomas, and Stan Winston. To Producers Lawrence Gordon, Joel Silver, and John Davis. To the actors: Shane Black, Elpidia Carrillo, Richard Chaves, Bill Duke, Kevin Peter Hall, Sonny Landham, Arnold Schwarzenegger, Jesse Ventura, and Carl Weathers. I prefer them in alphabetical order, even if that's not the way the credits work (you probably wouldn't be surprised to know that there are very specific, negotiated rules for the order of end credits after movies). I really want to shout out Stan Winston again for the Predator. The movie and this book and my life would be much poorer without it. To Alan Silvestri, too, for the music, and Little Richard for infiltrating the score.

Thanks to Paul Monette for the novelization and so much beautiful work. I started out with just the factoid of the novelization and ended up reading everything. Thanks to whoever presented on *Love Alone* in Joel Brouwer's poetry workshop in Spring 2001 for bringing the novelization to my attention. And particular thanks to David Groff and the Bresnick Weil Literary Agency, St. Martin's Press, Mariner Books, and all of Paul's publishers for allowing me to quote from his journals and work.

This book would not have been completed in this form without a fellowship from the Guggenheim Foundation. I am deeply grateful for your confidence and for allowing me to tell everyone I got a Guggenheim to write about *Predator*, surely a first (and I hope not a last).

Thanks to my editor Katie Dublinski, who knew how to help pull me from the depths of my obsession and produce this book instead. Thanks too to Jacqueline Ko, for your belief and support and guidance. I also owe thanks to the team of crack commandos at Graywolf, especially Chantz Erolin, Jeff Shotts, Fiona McCrae, and everyone else who believed in publishing this weirdo book.

Thanks to my strike team in Arizona: Kate Bernheimer, Susan Briante, Maritza Cardenas, Alison Deming, Paul Hurh, Reed Karaim, Bojan Louis, Farid Matuk, Clint McCall, Manuel Muñoz, Jon Reinhardt, Aurelie Sheehan, and Nicole Walker.

Thanks to my brother Ben, with whom I watched most of these movies. "Remember when I said I'd kill you last? / I lied."

Thanks to my father, Terry, my mother, Judy, and my stepmother, Paula, for all the parenting (which is most of it, obviously) that wasn't done by *Predator*. It was and is substantial. This book proves it, I hope.

Thanks to comrades in arms through the years, including Ryan, Matt, Jerry, Jeremiah, Dane, Graham, Rob, and Chris. I'm feeling very confident I'm forgetting someone—probably many someones. I'll have to make it up to you later, like always.

To our three predators who died during the making of this book— Napoleon, Rooster, and Toulouse—and to their three successors— Jax, Frank, and Samantha.

Thanks to Jim Sorenson for the Predator countdown font and to Jacob Slichter for the conversation.

Excerpts from this book—often in *very* different iterations—have appeared in a number of journals, including: *45th Parallel, Dusie,*

Eleven Eleven, *Midwest Review*, *Phoebe*, the *Spectacle*, *Speculative Nonfiction*, *Terrain.org*, *Texas Review*, *Tin House*, and *TriQuarterly*.

Another excerpt appeared in *Still Life with Poem*, ed. Jehanne Dubrow and Lindsay Lusby.

Many thanks to these editors for your willingness to roll with the Predator.

Quotations from Paul Monette's *Becoming a Man: Half a Life Story* (1992) are courtesy of Harper Perennial. Those from *Borrowed Time: An AIDS Memoir* (1988) are from Mariner Books. Those from *Love Alone* (1988) are courtesy St. Martin's Press. Those from *Predator* (1987) are courtesy Virgin Books.

You should definitely read Monette's novelization of *Predator*. For all its flaws, it's the best novelization I've read. The *Alien* ones are also good. Brian Evenson wrote a great book in the *Alien* universe, and don't sleep on Jeff VanderMeer's *Predator: South China Sea*. It rules.

Quotations from Paul Monette's journals are used by permission of the Monette Estate. Thanks to the librarians at UCLA special collections and everywhere who keep the torches lit.

ANDER MONSON is the author of eight previous books: four of non-fiction (*Neck Deep and Other Predicaments, Vanishing Point, Letter to a Future Lover*, and *I Will Take the Answer*), two poetry collections (*Vacationland* and *The Available World*), and two books of fiction (*Other Electricities* and *The Gnome Stories*). A finalist for the New York Public Library Young Lions Award (for *Other Electricities*) and a National Book Critics Circle Award in criticism (for *Vanishing Point*), he is also a recipient of a number of other prizes: a Howard Foundation Fellowship, the Graywolf Press Nonfiction Prize, the Annie Dillard Award for Nonfiction, the Great Lakes Colleges New Writers Award in Nonfiction, and a Guggenheim Fellowship. He edits the magazine *DIAGRAM* (thediagram.com), the New Michigan Press, Essay Daily (essaydaily.org), and a series of yearly literary/music tournaments: March Sadness (2016), March Fadness (2017), March Shredness (2018), March Vladness (2019), March Badness (2020), March Plaidness (2021), and March Faxness (2022). He lives in Arizona.

More at otherelectricities.com.

The text of *Predator* is set in Minion Pro.
Book design by Rachel Holscher.
Composition by Bookmobile Design and Digital
Publisher Services, Minneapolis, Minnesota.
Manufactured by Kingery Printing on acid-free,
100 percent postconsumer wastepaper.